Beyond the
Observatory *

BEYOND THE OBSERVATORY

Harlow Shapley

Charles Scribner's Sons

New York

Printed in the United States of America
Library of Congress Catalog Card Number 67-14493
SBN 684-31120-8 (Trade cloth)
SBN 684-12740-7 (Trade paper, SL)

Contents *

Contents

6 ✱

Foreword *

THESE informal essays, several of them developed from talks I have given over the past few years, deal with a variety of topics, more of them in the realm of practical sociology than in that of astronomy, and with much intermingling of disciplines. For if we would contemplate the colossal galaxies, we must approach by way of wavelengths—the minutest of measured things; and if we would contemplate the neutrinos, we should give thought to the endless space-time world in which such elementary particles are embedded.

Among these essays some are dominantly biological. They are: "Life and Hope in the Psychozoic Era"; "Apologies to a Comet"; "The Five Beasts of My

Own Apocalypse." Some are astronomical: "Life Among the Dwarfs"; "Thirty Deductions from a Glimmer of Star Light." The remainder fall in the categories of general and social science.

There is in the essays some repetition, not of plain statements but of argument. For example, in two essays, "Breathing the Future and the Past" and "Six Notes on Planets and Life," I discuss the atomic element argon, once to relate it to the evolution of the elements and once to emphasize the "sociology" of the many species of atoms.

We may look with amazement, and in fact with pride, at the list of ten revelations in the first essay. Have we come to the end of the sensational developments that have done much to orient man's thinking and doing? Most certainly not! Tremendous achievements have already been made in space exploration, and I would be inclined to predict even bigger and faster equipment and exploitation of space in further new and strange ways.

In the field of cosmography, what about the recently discovered quasars and other queer objects that seem to be millions of times bigger than the stars and a billion times brighter? There is something mysterious here that transcends the present theories about galaxies and their spaces.

By way of some new kind of chemistry, the mystery of the origin of life may be solved in the near future.

There are, I believe, scientific discoveries just ahead that will help to revise our knowledge of space, time, and matter.

It is indeed a grand time to be alive and asking questions.

HARLOW SHAPLEY

1 *

Ten Revelations

*that have most affected modern
man's life and thought*

THE universe of galaxies is expanding at a terrific rate, doubling its dimensions every few hundred years. But the universe of human knowledge is now doubling every decade. We are living in the midst of an intellectual explosion. This outburst of information about the world and ourselves is spectacular and stimulating. The physical and biological sciences, and the social sciences as well, are now amazingly alert. I shall enumerate, without immediate explanation, the ten revelations or achievements of the twentieth century which seem to me to have most profoundly affected the lives and thoughts of mankind. Since this listing refers to the present century only, radioactivity, the origin of species (Darwinism), and spectrum analysis are not included.

1. Knowledge of the chemistry of life's origin

2. Cosmic evolution—neutrons to man and beyond

3. Relativity theories—special and general

4. The corpuscular sciences

5. Automation and computers (cybernetics)

6. Space exploration

7. Galaxies, quasars, and the expanding universe

8. Medical triumphs

9. Molecular biology—viruses and DNA

10. Exploration of the mind

All those were sensational achievements and they continue to be epochal. When they are examined in detail each in turn appears to be the most important. Some are quite independent. Some, however, would not have been possible but for the previous appearance of one or more of the others. Cosmic evolution depends on relativity; medical triumphs depend on corpuscular sciences.

Keeping in mind that our survey of achievements is restricted to this century and to matters scientific, we can usefully review the list, giving a brief explanation to each revelation.

1. By "the origin of life" I mean the transition from the lifeless to the living, from the inanimate to the animate. Life can be defined in its simplest form as the continuous activity of self-replicating macromolecules. Formerly the origin of the animate was held to be a matter for the Deity to take care of; it was a field for miracles and the supernatural. But no longer. Philosophy and religion, and probably ethics, are profoundly affected by the recent explorations in molecular biology and galactic astronomy.

2. Cosmic evolution: nothing seems to be more important philosophically than the revelation that the evolutionary drive, which has in recent years swept over the whole field of biology, also includes in its sweep the evolution of galaxies, and stars, and comets, and

atoms, and indeed all things material. Man in his vaunted superiority is but a minute though interesting detail in the cosmic opera wherein we all play minor parts.

3. The discovery of the relativity of space, time, matter, and energy—that is, the tying together of those basic entities by way of Einstein's vision—must always stand as a supreme achievement by the groping mind of man. The popular and dreadful equation, $E = mc^2$, which says that Energy (E) is the same as mass (m) when the velocity of light (c) is introduced, is only one part of the relativity reformation.

4. Corpuscular sciences and technologies: the many particles of the atomic underworld—we call them corpuscles sometimes, and sometimes fundamental particles—deeply affect our lives and our modern living. The corpuscular sciences include those dealing with X rays, quanta, lasers, radioactivity, cosmic

rays, radio, and television—all very practical and all full of the future.

5. Automation, computers, cybernetics—an area in which the hard sciences join with sociology and the humanities to affect directly the lives and thoughts of men—are remarkably significant. For example, an inventor sees how human labors might be softened, abbreviated, or altogether eliminated, and he boldly gets to work—boldly on the principle that Audacity is the Mother of Success. At the heart of automatic operations are the throbbing, scintillating computers with their transistors that have opened a new world of information getting and information analyzing.

6. Long ago, the first Sputnik had forerunners aloft. In early centuries, air travelers were largely mythical. Some were biblical characters. From Daedalus and Icarus of Greek mythology to man-carrying balloons and jet travel of today there have been bold explorers of the at-

mospheric medium. The German war rockets marked the practical beginning of man's big attack on the ramparts of extraterrestrial space. The American Robert Goddard was a pioneer in rocket building. The astronauts of the present time have reached the moon and are heading for the planets. Venus and Mars have become magnificent targets. Planetary landings are among the greatest challenges that have been offered since the beginning of human curiosity.

7. Galaxies, a few decades ago, were hazy patches of light concerning which we had only hazy notions, or no thoughtful interpretation at all. Now they are recognized as stupendous accumulations of stars, one of which we conceitedly call "our" galaxy. Man, the so-called crowning glory of Creation, is revealed to be peripheral, off-center, in one galaxy among uncounted millions. The whole world of galaxies—now called the metagalaxy—is expanding in all directions.

8. Medical triumphs: human misery

has in this century yielded in spectacular ways to the biological attack on the major diseases of man and beast. The story can be briefly and dramatically presented by simply writing down the following pregnant words: diphtheria, smallpox, tuberculosis, polio, cholera, yellow fever, vaccination, sulfa, penicillin.

9. Molecular biology: in the biological underworld the viruses and DNA (deoxyribonucleic acid) do what the corpuscles do for microcosmic physics. Instead of quanta, electrons, and their like, we are here dealing with germs, bacteria, and their like. We are considering life at its lowest. We concern ourselves with amino acids and nucleic acids, and with chromosomes that carry the essence of genetics.

10. Exploration of the mind: Sigmund Freud and his dreams appear to have brought into the mental world about as much excitement, confusion, and doubt as Albert Einstein, Niels

Bohr, and Werner Heisenberg first brought into atomic physics. But much has now been straightened out by the introduction of clarifying subhypotheses. Some would say that the tenth revelation is the most important of all. Others might propose that there is already too much nonsense at large.

Now the stage is set and we can proceed to examine some of our revelations in more detail. But first we should observe that there are revelations other than those included in this codex of ten items. These others, however, fit so neatly into the foregoing scheme that they do not require separate entries. For example, for one reason or another, we do not list separately human-population control, Mössbauer radiation, Keynesian economics, or radio astronomy. These are included clearly enough in other categories or are as yet too little known to be influential.

The first of the ten items and the last

three are basically biological. They may seem a shade less significant than the others. But no! The discovery that life appears to be an *inevitable* occurrence when the physics, chemistry, and climatology are right leads directly to our deepest thoughts. A top position for the origin of life must be retained. Nor are numbers 8, 9, and 10 too local and anthropocentric. We shall keep them.

Life and the living of it is a desperately complicated business. The full analysis of the interior of a butterfly larva is vastly more difficult than the analysis of the interior of the remote star Polaris. For the insect we must deal with matter in gaseous, liquid, and solid states, whereas the interior of the North Star concerns only gas and radiation— no solids, no liquids.

The fossils in the rocks give us a start on the problem of the origin of life. They show that the beginning of living things was not recent. Man's ancestors date back a mere million years or so—

that is, those ancestors that we are willing to call men. But the great lizards, such as Brontosaurus, were splashing around in the Mesozoic swamps a hundred million years ago, and the lowly trilobites were leaving their records in the Paleozoic rocks half a billion years ago in the dim past.

The actual origin of the living forms from which we animals and plants descended, was much further back, probably in the times when the hot rocks of the young earth were cooling off and the atmosphere was chiefly composed, not of nitrogen and oxygen as it is now, but of methane, ammonia, water vapor, and hydrogen gas.

In those days, the same as now, there was abundant water in a liquid state which is necessary for the kind of life we practice. But how did we get started? Did life in the form of plant spores travel here from other planets? That suggestion dates back about a hundred years, before we knew about cosmic rays in interstellar space, and micrometeorites, and lethal ultraviolet radiation. The current belief is that the most primitive organisms were developed right here on the earth. The gaseous atmosphere of the cooling earth, when radiated by lightning, could get us started. One secret of our success was the absence from the atmosphere of oxygen in gaseous form. At that time there was actually much oxygen on the surface of the earth—about 50 percent of the earth's rocky crust is oxygen and 25 percent is silicon. But from the beginning the oxygen was tied up in the silicon rocks (SiO_2) and in water (H_2O). Gradually, however, free oxygen appeared in the atmosphere. Part of it was released from water as a result of short-wave solar radiation playing on the water vapor that had drifted to the top of the atmosphere. Later, after plants appeared, oxygen was also released into the air by photosynthesis which broke down carbon dioxide (CO_2).

From a reducing atmosphere, dominated by hydrogen, there evolved slowly an oxidizing atmosphere. (Raw oxygen would be lethal to timidly emerging experiments in early protoplasmic life.) This was the time when life could begin and could get tough enough to withstand the burning by oxygen.

In summary, life originated on or in the shallow waters of Pre-Cambrian days, some three or four billion years ago—originated and persisted. The primeval gases—methane, ammonia, water vapor, hydrogen gas, and one or two others—were radiated by ultraviolet sunlight; also by gamma rays from decaying elements such as radium, uranium, and potassium; also by geyser heat; and especially by lightning. Thanks to the billions of years available for the experiment, the amino acids, viruses, nucleic acids, and other chemical compounds formed, and these syntheses got life started. From the first, Darwinian principles took hold and produced by successive mutations the million kinds of plants and animals that now exist on this planetary surface. Our presence here is evidence that when the physics, chemistry, and climate are propitious, life will naturally emerge and persist.

From the origin and evolution of life forms, we now turn to cosmic evolution.

Betelgeuse and Antares are enormous red stars; Rigel and Vega are bluish and of average size; the sun is a yellowish star, intermediate in color, in temperature, and probably in age. Given time enough, will Betelgeuse get smaller or Vega become red? Will one type evolve into something like the other? A few detached notes will provide some guidance to our thinking about nonbiological evolution.

In compiling her great catalogues of stellar spectra, positions, and brightness in the early twentieth century, Miss Annie Cannon at the Harvard Observatory set up more than fifty types of spectra. All types of stars are radiating their materials into the deep freeze of interstellar space. There can no longer be doubt that evolution prevails throughout the stellar universe. In the act of shining the sun is losing matter at the rate of 4 million tons per second, and therefore it is steadily losing its energy content. It is evolving. The same holds for other stars; by shining, all the stars evolve. Some red stars are young, some old. Some supergiant yellowish stars are ten thousand times as bright as the sun. Other yellow stars are compact.

Does the evolutionary principle also touch star clusters, and galaxies of stars? The answer is that everything material in interstellar space evolves, but only recently have we become aware of the wide spread of this nonbiological evolution.

Some living forms change rapidly.

Others, like certain marine plants, are relatively stable over the millennia. Dinosaurs ran their spectacular course in about a hundred million years; some cockroaches have been on earth and not much changed for twice as long. The algae and fungi of the present time look and live much like those of half a billion years ago. Sometimes it is fast, sometimes slow, but evolution is certain.

Stellar evolution also implies that a planet such as the earth or Venus evolves from a whirling gaseous mass to a pretty solid affair that has lost its hydrogen and helium and other fast-moving light-weight gases. In fact, by way of its volcanoes and earthquake adjustments, our planet is still changing.

While there are many types of galaxies, the dominant ones are the spirals, the spheroidals, and the irregulars. Since all their billions of individual stars evolve, so too the galaxies must change with time—in mass, in luminosity, in motion, and in organization.

Since the evidence is now strong that evolution has affected galaxies, stars, planets, nebulae, comets, and meteor streams, and as a side issue the biological world, including *Homo sapiens,* what have we left, I ask, that is unchangeable?

We might wonder about the clouds of galaxies and speculate that the total universe itself may be evolving according to some unknown law or tendency. The observed scattering of the galaxies suggests an evolutionary operation for which various explanations have been proposed—for example, the "Big Bang" hypothesis of Georges Lemaître and George Gamow; the Steady-State hypothesis of Herman Bondi, Thomas Gold, and Fred Hoyle; or the Pulsing Universe hypothesis suggested by Milton Humason's observations with the Hale reflector.

But leaving the Expanding Universe aside for the time being, let us go downward in dimensions and ask whether the chemical elements are unchangeable, or of they also evolve.

More than a century ago chemists noted that oxygen atoms are almost exactly sixteen times as heavy, atom for atom, as those of hydrogen. If you could somehow put 16 hydrogen atoms together you would have 1 atom of oxygen. If you put 12 hydrogen atoms together, you have 1 carbon atom; 14 would equal 1 nitrogen atom. A growth probability was suggested here, but the concept that hydrogen can evolve into the heavier elements was promptly spoiled when it was found that most elements do not have even-numbered atomic weights in terms of the hydrogen atom.

Times have changed rapidly. In this century we have learned that the presence of isotopes accounts for the uneven-numbered atomic weights. There are, for instance, several kinds of tin—about a dozen. Each kind has an even-numbered atomic weight, but the mixture of the kinds results in an uneven-numbered final weight.

So back we go to the thought that all the ninety-odd chemical elements and their isotopes are descendants of the basic element hydrogen, the simplest of all atoms. If so, evolution has gone all the way, from the hydrogen atom, which is about one-billionth of an inch in diameter, to the metagalaxy, which is more than 1000 million trillion miles in diameter.

Now we ask the grand questions: "What is the ancestor of the hydrogen atoms?" and "What is the destiny of the metagalaxy?" We ask the questions—get no reply!

In considering the evolution of all matter out of hydrogen and its descendants, we overlooked an important consideration: very high temperatures are required to make the transitions. Something like 10 million degrees centigrade is required to burn the hydrogen, H (fuel), into the helium, He (ash),)and thereby to make a most important evolutionary step.

The transformation formula is simple: $4H = 1 \, He + \gamma$. (That γ, gamma, is the mass-energy that can produce atomic bombs and other violences of the atomic age.) Four hydrogen atoms "weigh" a little more than one helium atom, and that little leftover mass, in the form of energy, is the power that runs the sun and most of the stars.

The temperature in the interior of the sun is high enough to cook hydrogen into helium, but not high enough to transform the helium into oxygen and the other ninety-odd elments. Fortunately, we now know how mutations that require more heat are managed. Occasionally stars get out of balance and blow up. We call such stars novae. The temperatures of such explosions are high enough to accomplish another step in atomic evolution by producing oxygen, but still not high enough to change oxygen atoms into iron atoms. Sometimes the explosion does more than blow off the surface gases. Sometimes—though rarely—a supernova explosion blows the star to smithereens, producing temperatures that are measured in billions of degrees. We have, therefore, in such explosions, temperatures sufficiently high to carry evolution to the heavier atoms. Many details in this operation are yet to be worked out. Meanwhile we put on record that the aforementioned *Homo sapiens* has been able to tie together the knowledge he has picked up here and there and come forth with the assurance that everything in the microcosmos and macrocosmos changes with time. Certainly it is appropriate to speak of cosmic evolution.

2 *

Breathing
the Future
and the Past

or life with the argon atom

I LIKE numbers, in a playful sort of way. I like counting. The number of fence-leaping sheep may induce my sleep. Or the number of deadly sins—seven, I believe. They are as soporific as a hundred jumping sheep, for each sin leads us down drowsy paths of retrospection. Or counting stars—those "innumerable, pitiless, passionate eyes." No, the stars are not numberless. In his census of the "tyrants in your iron skies," Alfred, Lord Tennyson, could see only three or four thousand, unless he resorted to gadgetry such as telescopes and photographs. Perhaps they looked uncountable to him because of their uncertain glimmering at the limit of vision.

To indulge ourselves in numbers in a big way we need to enter the realm of stars and light-years, or go down into the microcosmic world of atoms. Why not count the atoms in a single deep breath of, say, Cleopatra, or the thought cells in the forebrain of an Einstein. Not easy, but it can be done! For Cleopatra's single breath it would require 1000 men counting 100 atoms a second, 8 hours a day, for about 10 billion years. They could be better employed.

The number of molecules of H_2O in a drop of water is staggering. When I report that it is a million times a million, provided that the water drop is *very* small, I am emphasizing not the greatness of the water drop but the minuteness of a molecule.

Let us look for a moment at a single ordinary water molecule. In a sense it would be an intimate introspection, for there are more water molecules in the reader's body than molecules of all other kinds. As the formula H_2O shows, and everyone knows, the water molecule is a system composed of 2 atoms of hydrogen and 1 of oxygen. The hydrogen atom is simply 1 electron circling 1 proton. The oxygen atom is composed of 8 protons and 8 neutrons packed in a nucleus, and

8 speedily circling electrons. We shall not pause to explain further the atomic building blocks that compose all matter —the electrons, protons, and neutrons. We are not quite able to do so. Scientists know better what these "corpuscles" do than what they are. We might say that electrons are chunks of negative electricity, protons are chunks of positive electricity, and neutrons are just chunks. Together with some evanescent corpuscles, they constitute the ninety-two kinds of essentially stable atoms.

In this sketch I propose to present briefly the science and romance of one of those kinds of atoms. It is argon. But first a little more about atoms in general.

I am being fair enough to the reader, I believe, if I invite him to indulge in serious thought about the underworld of atoms, for we are living in an amazing atomic age. We are, or should be, atom-minded.

Thirty years ago, while undergoing

✳ 37

experimentation in our laboratories, the uranium atom broke down; we now have, as a result of its splitting, the A-bomb, the atom-fueled submarine, and some atom-produced electric current in our light and power lines. We have the Atomic Age—a new, exciting era in the progress of civilization.

Not long after the first fission of the uranium atom came the still more horrendous fusion of hydrogen. In consequence there emerge the H-bomb and the multi-billion-dollar budgets that seem so necessary to defend us against ourselves. Certainly we should be atomconcious, for those tiny chunks of energy carry a mighty wallop and are writing the future of mankind.

The various kinds of atoms not only have names, many of them have familiar names—such as tin, gold, sulfur, iron, and radium. We have also assigned them specific numbers from 1 to more than 100. The numbering is in order of increasing weight and complexity. Simple hydrogen is Atom no. 1. Its high distinction lies in the circumstance that with hydrogen fuel the universe has been cooked. The fact that so much hydrogen still remains in stars and in "empty" space assures a long radiant future for the sun, and incidentally for earthly life.

Helium, which is Atom no. 2, is four times as heavy as hydrogen. Lithium (no. 3) is a rather obscure type of atom compared, for instance, with carbon (no. 6), nitrogen (no. 7), and oxygen (no. 8). Argon, the principal subject of this essay, is no. 18. In its most common form argon is composed of 18 protons, 22 neutrons, and 18 electrons. The electrons are so distributed in the outer structure of the argon atom that other kinds of atoms cannot make combinations with it. There are no "handles" which other atoms can grasp and hold, as oxygen can grasp and hold 2 hydrogen atoms to produce the water molecule.

Oxygen is very hungry for atomic associations, and so is carbon. Their electron arrangements are wonderfully suited to the making of compounds. Carbon and hydrogen can make methane; carbon, oxygen, and hydrogen combine for various kinds of sugar; oxygen and nitrogen make laughing gas; oxygen and silicon form a compound that constitutes about three-fourths of the earth's crust; and so on, for thousands of compounds. But argon remains aloof; apparently it makes no compounds. It is inert. The same is true of helium and a few others—all of them with their circling electrons so organized that intimate association with other atoms is not possible.

The inert atom named argon (which is a Greek word meaning inactive) will not work, but, as I shall show, it does tie us up in a thought-provoking way with the dinosaurs, and the Last Supper, and the bombast of Adolf Hitler.

Back to the number game. We get from the astronomers (celestial mechanicians) the information that the small planet earth has a mass of 6000 million trillion tons. That mass includes rocks, oceans, lakes, rivers, and the atmosphere. About one-millionth is the earth's atmosphere, which would weigh in at the earth's surface at a robust 6000 trillion tons. We could also express that number as 6 million billion tons. Or we could use a more compact terminology and say the the tonnage of air is 6×10^{15}, which means 6 followed by 15 zeros.

For more than a century chemists have known that the earth's envelope of air is composed almost entirely of just two gases, nitrogen and oxygen. But about a century ago the researches by Lord John Rayleigh and Sir William Ramsay indicated that there must be something else in the air. Those gifted British scientists had noted, of course, that there is some water vapor in the air, mostly in the clouds, also a slight amount of carbon dioxide, coming from the breathing of animals and from the breath of volcanoes, but that degree of pollution does not amount to much in the sum total of the earth's atmosphere.

The H_2O and CO_2 were removed by Ramsay and Rayleigh for their experimental work. When dry clean air was analyzed they found that about 1 percent of the whole atmosphere could be attributed to some other transparent gas, theretofore unknown. Isolating and analyzing this residue gas, they discovered that the new element is inert, that its atoms are about forty times as heavy as hydrogen atoms, and that it is a part of all terrestrial air, diffused uniformly over the earth's surface and probably extending up a hundred miles and more to the top of the atmosphere. Of necessity this gas is involved in all animal breaths, along with nitrogen and oxygen.

Ramsay and his colleagues pursued their study of air and eventually found, in extremely small quantities, the other inert gases—helium, neon, krypton, xenon, and radon. Sir William named them the "noble" gases in jesting reference to the traditional aloofness and idleness of the nobility!

Nitrogen is not very active in combining with other kinds of atoms to form compounds—it is semi-inert. But oxygen, as we have mentioned, is tremendously active in atomic associations. It is a most democratic element, joining up in myriads of ways, and indispensable for the common life. It is the oxygen of the air that we seek so dramatically in our cyclic breathing. Without our continuous intake of oxygen we would be finished off in a few minutes. We must have oxygen. But eliminate argon from the earth's atmosphere and we air-breathing animals would take no notice whatever of its absence.

How much of this idle argon is there in our gaseous envelope? An approximate value is slightly less than 1 percent of our whole atmosphere—that is, it totals 6×10^{13} tons—60 trillion tons. The

✳ 43

total number of argon atoms in the whole terrestrial atmosphere is an incomprehensible 10^{42}.

Thanks to the mobility of gases, the winds at the earth's surface keep the atmosphere thoroughly stirred up and in motion. Here today, gone tomorrow, are the atoms that we are now breathing. The atomic mixture remains uniform with respect to the three main components, by weight nitrogen 76 percent, oxygen 23 percent, argon 1 percent. Near the earth's surface the nitrogen and oxygen are in *molecular* form: we symbolize them as N_2 and O_2. Near the top of the atmosphere these gases are in *atomic* form, N_1 and O_1, because the energy of sunlight breaks each molecule into two atoms. The argon of the atmosphere is always in atomic form, and its atomic weight and atomic motions are such that the earth's gravity does not permit its escape from the earth into interplanetary space. In the composition of the sun and most other stars hydrogen

and helium together make up more than
99 percent.

Since about 1 percent of your breath
is argon we can determine approximately the number of atoms in your
next argonic intake. The calculations
are really rather simple and straightforward, but to some readers this dizzy
arithmetic is repulsive and I shall simply
state the results. In your next determined
effort to get oxygen to your lungs and
tissues—that is, in your next breath—
you are taking in, besides the nitrogen
and oxygen, 30,000,000,000,000,000,000,
atoms of argon; in briefer statement 3×10^{19}. (Count the zeros!) A few seconds
later you exhale those argon atoms
along with quintillions of molecules of
carbon dioxide. The plants will appreciate your carbon dioxide molecules and
make vital use of them when sunlight
and chlorophyll do their magic of putting the carbon into the plant tissues
and releasing the oxygen into the air

where we breathing animals can use it for our living.

A wonderfully effective cooperation is going on in this atomic exchange—the animals, such as you, breathe out carbon dioxide for the plants; the plants release oxygen for the animals, which again serve the plants with carbon dioxide, which then serve oxygen to the animals. . . . A biological barter economics is in operation, with carbon and oxygen atoms serving as units of exchange, along with sunlight.

If the plants were completely removed from the surface of the earth, the atmospheric oxygen would soon disappear because it would all be absorbed into the soil and rocks. With the oxygen decreasing, all the animals would gradually smother. On the other hand, if animal life were entirely removed from the earth, the plants would have to depend skimpily on the carbon dioxide of volcanoes and of organic decay. Animals and plants need each other vitally.

Now let us follow the career of one argon-rich breath—your next exhalation, let us suppose. We shall call it Breath X. It quickly spreads. Its argon, exhaled this morning, by nightfall is all over the neighborhood. In a week it is distributed all over the country; in a month, it is in all places where winds blow and gases diffuse. By the end of the year, the 3×10^{10} argon atoms of Breath X will be smoothly distributed throughout all the free air of the earth. You will then be breathing some of those same atoms again. A day's breathing a year from now, wherever you are on the earth's surface, will include at least 15 of the argon atoms of today's Breath X.

This rebreathing of the argon atoms of past breaths, your own and others', has some picturesque implications. The argon atoms associate us, by an airy bond, with the past and the future. For instance, if you are more than twenty years old you have inhaled more than 100 million breaths, each with its appall-

* 47

ing number of argon atoms. You contribute so many argon atoms to the atmospheric bank on which we all draw, that the first little gasp of every baby born on earth a year ago contained argon atoms that you have since breathed. And it is a grim fact that you have also contributed a bit to the last gasp of the perishing.

Every saint and every sinner of earlier days, and every common man and common beast, have put argon atoms into the general atmospheric treasury. Your next breath will contain more than 400,000 of the argon atoms that Gandhi breathed in his long life. Argon atoms are here from the conversations at the Last Supper, from the arguments of diplomats at Yalta, and from the recitations of the classic poets. We have argon from the sighs and pledges of ancient lovers, from the battle cries at Waterloo, even from last year's argonic output by the writer of these lines, who personally has had already more than 300 million breathing experiences. Our next

48 ✳

breaths, yours and mine, will sample the snorts, sighs, bellows, shrieks, cheers, and spoken prayers of the prehistoric and historic past.

There was a time when very little argon existed in the earth's atmosphere, and practically no free oxygen at all. That was some billions of years ago. The oxygen has been built up to its present abundance on the earth by the breathing of green plants, and the argon, over the millennia, has grown to its present percentage as the result of the radioactivity of one of the isotopes of the potassium atoms of the rocks. That radioactive decay steadily goes on. In 5 billion years our atmosphere will contain about twice as much argon as it does now.

There ought to be a moral to this story of argon. It tells us of the dramatic smallness of the units of matter. It reminds us of the turbulence in the healthful gaseous envelope which we call our

✳ 49

atmosphere. It associates us intimately with the past and the future. It argues that to live long and naturally we want to have in our atmosphere only salutary atoms—oxygen, nitrogen, and argon. We do not want to have this mixture corrupted, polluted, poisoned. Therefore we do not want to have anywhere in our atmosphere the man-made atoms of strontium-90, iodine-131, and similar artifacts produced by ingenious but shortsighted man.

The moral could be: Respect your breath! Keep it decent!

3 *

Life Among the Dwarfs

EVERYBODY now knows much about the moon, its mountains, its valleys, its barrenness; but some of the so-called knowledge is as farfetched as the old green-cheese notion—for example, the alleged effect of the moon's phases on the weather and on field crops. That the moon circles the earth is a common statement. In a sense, yes, it does; but the words "circles" and "earth" are inexact. More accurately, the moon moves in an elongated orbit, not a circle, and it goes monthly around the center of gravity of the earth-moon pair, not around the earth's center. (We could properly call this earth-moon pair a double planet.)

The gravitational center of the earth-moon system is on the line joining the centers of the two bodies, but because the earth is about eighty times as massive as the moon, the pair's center of mass is one-eightieth of the moon's distance

✳ 53

from the center of the earth; it is a thousand miles. below the earth's surface.

If the earth and the moon were of equal mass, the gravity center would be out in the open, equally distant from the two bodies. There are stars like that. Many double stars are composed of identical twins. But more often these stellar pairs are like the earth-moon system; they have a dominating member—dominating in size or brightness or both. The famous eclipsing star Algol in the constellation Perseus is such a one, as also are Sirius, the Dog Star; and Procyon, the Little Dog Star; and also giant Polaris at the North Pole of the sky.

These facts lead to a consideration of the general phenomenon of stellar doubling, and thence to knowledge of the existence, in these unequal pairs, of dwarfs among the heavenly bodies. More than half of the now known nearby stars are members of double or multiple systems. Probably the same frequency of dwarfs and doubling prevails throughout the billion-starred Milky Way.

Exploring deeply into space, beyond the bounds of our Milky Way galaxy, we come upon other galaxies, and among them we find double and triple systems, and indeed clusters of galaxies, gravitationally organized and operating. The gigantic, much-photographed Andromeda Nebula (Messier 31), which is a galaxy containing more than 100 billion stars, has two companion galaxies (Messier 32 and N.G.C. 205).* It is therefore a triple system, which is composed of one giant galaxy, one dwarf, and one of median size and population. More than that, this triple system is a member of a cluster of galaxies of which our own Milky Way and a dozen other

* Messier numbers are given in the catalogue of nebulae compiled in the eighteenth century by the French astronomer Charles Messier. N.G.C. 205 is also a catalogue number.

galaxies are also members. The Magellanic Clouds, well-known irregularly shaped galaxies in the southern hemisphere, are in this local cluster, and since they are only some 160,000 light-years away, they can be examined in detail with the larger telescopes of the southern hemisphere.

The million-galaxy survey at the Harvard Observatory, which I initiated long ago, and the surveys in California with the Mount Wilson, Palomar, and Lick Observatory telescopes all show that the physical clustering of galaxies is common practice throughout the metagalaxy—that is, throughout our galaxy of galaxies. In fact, most galaxies appear to be members of loose groupings, but some are in compact assemblies of hundreds.

So this is the organizational picture: myriads of giant and dwarf galaxies associated in pairs, multiples, and clusters; millions of giant and dwarf stars associated in pairs, multiples, and clusters;

and right here at home a double planet
—the earth and the moon.

I have mentioned Sirius, which is the
brightest star in the sky. What a peculiar
object it is! A little more than 8 light-
years distant, it appears at first glance to
be a typical single white-hot star. Its
nearness is responsible for its appearing
so bright. There are millions of stars in
the Milky Way that look much like Sirius. Have they also star-sized compan-
ions? Or do they have planetary systems
like that of our sun? We cannot be certain. The distances are too great and the
glare of the primaries interferes too
much for a successful search for faint
secondaries.

But the relative nearness of Sirius per-
mits a closer examination. We find that
the faint companion, called Sirius B, is a
dwarf star of very low candle power; Sirius A, the component we see so clearly,
is more than a thousand times as luminous. Sirius A and Sirius B revolve
around their common center of gravity

twice a century. Their orbits are elongated (elliptical) and only at their greatest distance from each other (apastron) can they be seen or photographed separately. Sirius B, although faint in appearance, and as small in volume as the earth, is packed full of matter so condensed that a handful from its center would weigh many tons. Sirius A is composed of normal matter—the atoms on its surface are full-sized, as on the earth and in the earth. Sirius B, however, is a white dwarf, composed, except near the surface, of collapsed atoms. Degenerate matter, we call it. The surface temperatures of both components are about 10,000 degrees centigrade, too hot for any kind of protoplasmic life. Protein molecules, such as those of which animal and plant cells are made, and inorganic molecules, such as those that compose rocks and oceans, would on those hot surfaces be dissociated into atoms, protons, and electrons.

There is, however, another kind of

dwarf star, where temperatures are not too high for many kinds of molecules. These are the reddish, relatively cool objects that I call Lilliputians (from *Gulliver's Travels*), because of their small size, and it is with them that this exploration is particularly concerned.

Because a wide range in the candle power of stars exists, we are likely to misjudge our neighbors. The stars we can see without telescopic aid are nearly all brighter than our sun. The stars that are actually nearest to us are nearly all much less luminous than the sun and are seen with difficulty.

In a given volume of space, say, the space within 16 light-years of the sun (100 trillion miles), we find more than fifty stars fainter than the sun and only two or three slightly more luminous. The most numerous stars in space are therefore not the kind we see with the naked eye, but rather the dwarfs and the subdwarfs of low luminosity. Recent studies, especially those of Willem J.

Luyten at the University of Minnesota, have suggested that the smaller the candle power the more numerous the dwarfs may be.

We have long known the remarkable fact that space around us is richly populated by dwarf stars, reddish and whitish, but we have not given much thought to the logical conclusion that (whatever the natural origin of stars) as the size and brightness decrease, the numbers increase. Some red dwarfs are but one-millionth of the sun's luminosity. They can be photographed, and spectra made with the large telescopes, only when they are near; they do not appear in the standard star catalogues. If they are very faint, the dwarf stars will be planetary in size and will not shine at all in ordinary light. These are the Lilliputians previously mentioned—probably very abundant in our neighborhood. Being small in mass, as well as in radiation, they have little or no measurable gravitational effect on the sun's planets, or on the motions of stars, or on the rotation of the galaxy.

If a Lilliputian should drift near to our planetary system, would we easily detect it? Not at first; but if unexplainable perturbations in the orbital motions of the planets should be discovered, we might charge these perturbations to the gravitational pull of a nearby unseen Lilliputian. And of course a really close approach to the solar system by a Lilliputian would eventually result in its becoming visible—that is, in its reflecting sunlight. Its brightness would depend on its nearness to the sun and to the observer on the earth.

Our sun is about ten times as great as Jupiter in diameter—a thousand times greater in volume. It is actually more than 430,000 miles in radius and is so massive that the internal temperature exceeds 10 million degrees centigrade— so hot from compression that deep in the solar interior the hydrogen of which

✳ 61

it is mostly composed is burning, leaving helium ash. The radiation from that hot interior is intense and of very short wavelength. The wavelength increases as the radiation "leaks" to the surface; it comes out to us and to surrounding space as the ordinary beneficent sunlight by grace of which we exist. And we shall, if we behave ourselves, continue to exist for billions of years—we plants and animals—for the sun has a great supply of stored hydrogen fuel, and its expenditure is nicely thermostated. If the sun should start to cool off, it would shrink and thereby raise the temperature; if it should start to heat up above the average condition, it would expand and lower the temperature. The fossil green algae of the Pre-Cambrian eras show us that the solar thermostat has been working steadily for a billion years and more.

Jupiter, Saturn, the earth, and the other solar-system planets have hot interiors produced by gravitational compression, but none of them has an internal temperature high enough to fuse hydrogen into helium as does our sun. Our earthly heat comes from three sources: from this ordinary compression which incites geysers and volcanoes; from the gamma radiation emitted by decaying radium, uranium, and potassium; and from sunlight, the last being the most effective.

Measurements of the temperature of Jupiter's atmosphere suggest that its allocation of sunshine is now its main heat source, but Jupiter is far from the sun, five times the earth-sun distance, and in consequence the temperature at Jupiter's surface is very low—colder than —100 degrees on the centigrade scale.

Is there any life on Jupiter? Not at the level in Jupiter's thick atmosphere where the low temperature is measured; probably nowhere above or below that atmospheric level, for planetary life as we know it requires water in a liquid state, neither as ice nor as superheated steam.

But suppose there were a planet ten times as massive as Jupiter. Its interior would be much hotter. And if it were fifty times as massive, the heat of gravitational compression would provide a warm surface. Then, if this were not too hot or too cold, there could be on the surface water in a liquid state. There could be conditions suitable for the evolution of giant molecules which are the forerunners of organisms.

These hypothetical giant self-warming Jupiters I call Brobdingnagian planets, carrying on the *Gulliver's Travels* nomenclature. Undoubtedly such bodies exist, not only in planetary systems that are hooked up with stars, but also as detached drifting bodies, remote from stars.

We now reckon from extensive sampling that there are *at least* one hundred thousand million billion stars in our universe; the number of attached planets must be similarly great, and probably there are many more planets in the detached category.

Life Among the Dwarfs

In this tremendous universe, the possible richness of life is much increased if we accept two hypotheses: first, that big planets can be sufficiently self-warming for protoplasmic experiments; and, second, that dwarf stars can be so dwarf, and so cooled off, that rocky crusts and watery surfaces can form on them and life evolve. Many of the red dwarfs are called "flare stars" because they occasionally erupt, producing great short-lived geyser effects. Is not this flare activity a natural by-product of cooling off and does it not progress with crust formation?

A few relevant observations follow:

1. Our best tool for hunting down intermediate star-planets may be the radio telescope. It works with radio wavelengths ranging from 1 inch and a little less to 30 feet and more. Many hundred radio "sources" have been located and catalogued. Only a small proportion of them have been definitely assigned to peculiar galaxies, or identified with neb-

ulous remnants of exploded stars, **or** interpreted as galaxies in collision. Some may be exploding galaxies. And many may be our dwarf dwarfs.

The radiation from these Lilliputians must lie largely in the radio section of the electromagnetic spectrum. A great field opens for researches in tracking down the radio sources that are as yet unidentified. They must abundantly exist in the size-and-brightness intervals between big planets and subdwarf stars. Meanwhile the strange objects called quasars and blue galaxies have entered the metagalactic picture. They remain unexplained.

2. Elementary life is now commonly recognized as one of the natural phenomena in the evolution of matter—nothing supernatural about it. Soon such life will be easily produced in the test tube.

3. Since organic existence is a product of sunlight, moisture, and certain chemical elements, of which hydrogen,

carbon, nitrogen, phosphorus, and oxygen are the most significant, we surmise that life may emerge and exist not only in water and on land, but in atmospheres as well. We should remember this possible locale of elementary life since the Brobdingnagian planets may have very thick atmospheres, mostly of hydrogen, which not only dominates in the sun but is also the principal element in interstellar space.

4. We now believe that all the scores of kinds of atoms have evolved naturally (and in some places are now evolving) from hydrogen, the simplest of atoms. But what is its source?

In summary, it is proposed that sub-subdwarf stars are numerous, at least in parts of the Milky Way, this proposition holding whether planets originated in a contracting primeval dust-and-gas cloud or as the product of violent eruptions and collisions of stars.

The origin and persistence of innumerable detached plant-sized bodies seems inevitable. Certainly some of these Lilliputian stars will have the proper physics, chemistry, and climatology for the natural emergence of life. Such a protoplasmic operation can take place either on self-warming independent wandering planets, or on planets something like Jupiter, attached by gravitation to a radiating star.

The life on independent self-warming bodies of the mass and consequent temperature necessary for the existence of the indispensable liquid water would be strange indeed. The necessary energy would come mainly from deep within and would appear at the surface mostly as radiation in the radio section of the electromagnetic spectrum. There would be no abundant violet-to-red light, and the sense organs functioning as eyes in life forms would need to be tuned to radio waves.

A strange world we would find it, but strangeness is also common among life forms on this sun-heated planet: contrast, for example, microbes with whales, sequoias with bacteria, bees with sponges! All these are protoplasmic operations. All are products of the cosmic processes that evolve atoms, biological cells, plants, animals, and mankind.

4 *

Six Notes on
Planets and Life

In this sketch of some interesting characteristics of the local planetary system, I shall examine in brief detail the following six topics: The Moon as a Fossil Planet; Argonic and Other Atmospheres; The Venus Greenhouse; Ozone and Life; The Earth's Primeval Atmosphere; Life Comes as Oxygen Dominates.

To save time and minimize argument let us agree on a few relevant situations and facts, or near facts:

1. We agree that our traveling in space must be confined to this solar system because even the nearest stars are hopelessly far away. We may rocket various bits of hardware out beyond the grasp of the solar system's gravity; that would not be impossibly difficult. But to what avail is an attempt to travel all the way to the stars? Opposed to such an enterprise is the physics of the situation (great distances and the finite velocity

of light) , and also the physiology and sociology—for example, the brevity of human life as now managed.

2. We agree also that the same kinds of atoms are here and elsewhere; that there is a cosmos-wide distribution of all the chemical elements, with of course local variations in the relative abundances, as for instance between the sun and the earth. The sun is dominantly hydrogen; the earth dominantly oxygen, iron, and silicon.

3. We accept the existence of an evolutionary thread or trend that runs through the earth's biology, from protophyta to man (and in some places probably beyond man) . Biological evolution is only a sideline in the cosmic evolution that extends from hydrogen gas (and whatever was earlier) to the hundred other kinds of atoms, thence to molecules and molecular aggregates, to planets, to nebulae, stars, galaxies, and, in suitable spots, to protoplasmic life. Possibly my account of the origin of life

as I have outlined it elsewhere* will not be accepted by many without my first detailing the evidence and arguing the details. But cosmic evolution can be tentatively taken as a good hypothesis, the strength of which lies in the indication that no other supposition is at this moment tenable.

THE MOON AS A FOSSIL PLANET

Whether the moon is a natural child of the earth or was adopted from the cosmic muck in early times has little bearing on the great interest and tender care we now devote to this nearest of large astronomical bodies. We do not want the moon disrupted by a man-made hydrogen bomb or infected with earth-grown viruses and bacteria.

So much has been written, so much has been speculated, about this handy

* *Of Stars and Men* (rev. ed.; Boston: Beacon Press, 1964), chap. iv.

✱ 75

extraterrestrial body that I can add little that is fresh. The moon is dry, essentially airless, and alternately hot from sunlight and cold from its lack. It is both rough and smooth, with mountains relatively high but with slopes not as steep as photographs have led us to suppose. Unshielded by a competent atmosphere, the lunar surface, except on the steeper slopes, is dusty from meteoric bombardment throughout thousands of millions of years; but some writers assume the surface to be porous, and others speculate that the holes and cracks are treacherously filled with dust particles that have been and are now being scattered over the moon's surface by electric charges produced by the rain of protons from the sun. However, these speculations were not confirmed by the findings of soft-landing space craft, like the Russian Lunar-9 and the American Surveyor-1. Both reported a rather firm surface, which probably can be explained by the absence of an atmosphere. In the absence of air, dust particles must pack firmly and might even undergo a kind of cold-welding process.

Thanks to the mechanical agility of Russian and American engineers, the solution of the seemingly hopeless mystery of the back side of the moon has been broached. It is good that we did obtain those preliminary backside lunar photographs, since they assured us of the expected ruggedness, and perhaps confused those philosophers who have argued that we have no credible evidence that the moon has a back side.

The detailed physiography of the visible lunar surface is now well known to all readers and television viewers. Gradually photography with cameras orbiting the moon or making soft landings on the moon's surface will delineate more clearly the small cracks, holes, hills, and slopes. In this connection, a small beginning has already been made with Surveyor-1, Orbiter-1, Orbiter-2, and the Apollo landings. We shall, I believe, eventually witness minor changes in surface details—changes arising from inner adjustments (moon quakes) and meteorite infall. But no major changes. The moon is a dead world. The rugged lunar surface shows us how the earth's surface appeared before it had been softened by the rains, winds, and vegetation. Such softeners are now and always have been absent on the moon's surface. On the earth, the craters made by meteor impact, of which the one in Arizona is best known, are not easily found; on the moon they are glaringly conspicuous.

ARGONIC AND OTHER ATMOSPHERES

Concerning the lunar atmosphere, there is nothing much to say. The original light-weight gaseous atoms promptly escaped to interplanetary space on the forming of our satellite. The surface gravity on the moon is too weak to hold high-speed atoms. The pressure of radiation from the sun, both by photons and protons, has assisted in cleaning the lunar surface of gas, but of course it was principally because the moon's surface gravity is so weak that the light-weight gases leaked away. The eclipsing of stars by the moon, as it moves across the sky, is so sudden that it confirms the moon's airlessness. However, further and more precise work on the light-drop for stars at the moon's edge must be undertaken to show how very little gas is there.

A deposit of oxygen gas on the moon's surface would soon disappear, some of it escaping into the vacuum of surrounding space, some of it going into the hungry rocks through absorption and chemical reaction. On the other hand, the gas argon, which was discussed earlier in this book, presents a different story. Like the other inert atoms it remains in gaseous form, even at the lowest temperatures on the moon, and does not combine with any other element. It is steadily produced at the moon's surface, probably, like most of the argon on the earth, coming from the natural radioactivity of one of the isotopes of potassium, which is a constituent of all kinds of rocks. When the radioactive potassium isotope of atomic weight 40 breaks down, stable calcium-40 is the principal end-product, but a small percentage appears as the stable gas argon-40. We have to do here with a natural atomic transmutation. When the argon gas is not held in the rocks from which it emerges, it will escape and become a thin lunar atmosphere. Meteors impinging on the lunar surface continually stir up the dust, exposing subsurface potassium and releasing argon gas.

The effectiveness of this potassium-argon operation is shown by the earth's present atmosphere, where the third most abundant atom is argon—by weight a full 1 percent of the earth's atmosphere. There are about 60 trillion

tons of argon now in the earth's atmosphere; it is thoroughly mixed, the earth
over, with the nitrogen and oxygen.
There must be argon also in the atmospheres of Mars and Venus, and everywhere else that potassium exists. The
earth holds its argon pretty well; the
moon does not, at least not permanently.

The continuously emerging argon is
of no use in human metabolic operations; moon travelers have to take their
life-saving oxygen with them or be pre-
pared to distill it out of rocks, where
there is much, and preserve it for
human breaths and other uses.

The other inert atoms—the lighter
ones are helium and neon, and the heavier ones, krypton, xenon, and radon—
provide altogether but one-thousandth
of 1 percent of the earth's atmosphere.
They do not have generous suppliers of
new atoms, as argon does. Some helium
is liberated by decaying radium, tho-
rium, and uranium, and there is indeed
evidence that xenon is very slowly in-

creasing through a radioactive feeder, an isotope of iodine; it **is** sufficiently heavy to be retained by the moon. But the increase in these atoms is negligible compared with the increase of argon. From the earth's atmosphere helium and even neon readily escape; the other inert gases do not. If we could check up on the amount of argon in the earth's atmosphere 4000 million years from now, we should find about 2 percent of it to be argon, twice the present value, while the amounts of the other inert gases would show little change.

The earth's atmosphere is therefore not unchangeable in composition. Its present constituents can be summarized as follows:

	PERCENT
Nitrogen	75.58
Oxygen	23.08
Argon	1.28
Other inert gases	0.001
Carbon dioxide	0.03
Water vapor, etc.	0.029

But not only is the argon undergoing an irreversible increase, the oxygen is also growing in amount as the spread of vegetation over the earth's surface increases. This spread may not be increasing rapidly at present because of the creeping deserts, but if the ingenuity of man changes the vast deserts (one-third of all land areas) to forests and green fields, photosynthesis will increase the atmospheric oxygen, absolutely and relatively.

Solar radiaton and the chlorophyll operation in green plants cooperate to release oxygen to the air by breaking down carbon dioxide and water. Animals, through their breathing, take free oxygen out of the air, and so does the rusting of surface rocks, while photosynthesis maintains the supply of oxygen. It is a nice symbiosis—plants and animals working the oxygen cycle.

If all vegetation were precipitately removed from the earth, the oxygen of the air would soon disappear into the rocks;

it would disappear most rapidly in an age of great volcanic activity when much unoxidized matter comes to the surface. This is probably what has happened on Mars—the original oxygen has rusted and reddened the surface rocks, and photosynthetic replenishment has been slight or nonexistent. The surface of Mars is essentially a hopeless desert, devoid of water and of the energy of free oxygen.

THE VENUS GREENHOUSE

So far we have been concerned with the surface of only one satellite, the moon, and the atmosphere of one planet, the earth. The earth and its sister planet, Venus (its twin sister, one might say), differ considerably, as can be seen by studying the comparative data in the table on pages 86-87.

We assume that the earth and Venus are of the same age, and of the same parentage. Their orbits are much alike. Yet Venus is severely cloud-bound, the earth nearly clear of clouds. Our planet's atmosphere is mostly nitrogen and oxygen; Venus's mostly nitrogen and carbon dioxide. The earth has a temperature variation and an agreeable climate that permit over most of its surface a remarkable protoplasmic adventure (life). Venus, on the other hand, is not agreeable. It has a surface temperature that according to recent radio telescope measures is above 800 degrees Fahrenheit. Such a temperature should make the space traveler hesitate about landing; he might find, as did Icarus before him, that near approaches to such hot spots as the sun would surely unglue him.

The reason for the considerable difference in surface conditions on the two similar planets may lie in some as yet undiscovered consequence of the earth's having a large satellite while Venus is moonless. Or it may lie in the slower

	DISTANCE FROM THE SUN (ASTRONOMICAL UNITS)	DIAMETER (MILES)	PERIOD OF REVOLUTION (YEARS)	PERIOD OF ROTATION (DAYS)
Earth	1.0	7913	1.0	1.0
Venus	0.72	7700	0.61	225 (?)

rotation of Venus (actual period not yet certainly known) which would affect both the solar radiation it receives and the reradiation. Or Venus may be without mountains, which certainly would affect its climate.

The present considerable degree of clarity of the earth's atmosphere could perhaps be explained by the hypothesis of the birth of the moon from the present Pacific Ocean. The consequent crustal deformations would have created high mountains and deep oceans which could seriously affect terrestrial climates.

However it may have come about, the dense and persistent cloud coverage of Venus acts like the glass of a greenhouse, transmitting the sun's radiant energy inward and holding it against the reradiation outward. Consequently the temper-

	RELATIVE MASS	MEAN DENSITY	MOONS	ESCAPE VELOCITY (MILES/SEC.)
Earth	1.0	5.52	1	7.0
Venus	0.81	4.86	none	6.3

ature rises to establish an equilibrium, which on the earth is attained at a much lower temperature than on Venus. The earth's atmosphere also acts as a blanket, keeping throughout the night much of the heat daily provided by the sun. Mars, because of its much thinner air blanket, has a considerably greater nightly drop of temperature. And our cloudless, blanketless moon cannot keep warm throughout its two weeks' long night, nor can barren Mercury. They are both waterless.

OZONE AND LIFE

The greatest atmospheric boon to life, next to the operation of photosynthesis, has been the formation in the earth's atmosphere of the gaseous ozone (O_3)

✳ 87

barrier. Without the blocking by ozone of the ultraviolet solar radiation, the kind of protoplasmic life we know might not have emerged in its many forms. But we should note that some other kind of organismic evolution might have developed in the presence of ultraviolet radiation (which is lethal to us) and attained to the self-replication that we associate with life. Such a circumstance is imaginable, though not realistic in view of what we now know of biochemistry.

This "other way up" from the inanimate to the living should be remembered when we consider the life possibilities on Mars. Its temperatures, its lack of oxygen as an energy source, its scarcity of water, and the absence of an ozone barrier must all be contended with. Terrestrial organisms, all the million forms, would doubtless perish promptly if Martian conditions were imposed on the earth. Naturally I recommend that we do not impose them, except in limited well-controlled

88 ✳

experiments, where they are important to space science and space travel.

The amount of ozone in our present atmosphere is quantitatively small, though very effective as a shield against radiations of wavelengths 3000 angstroms and less. Ozone is assisted in shielding animals and plants by other molecular compounds in the atmosphere. At the surface of the earth the ozone is negligible in amount, except when it is produced locally and transiently by lightning flashes. It is commonly present between 20 and 30 miles above the surface of the earth.

The ozone barrier in the earth's atmosphere may be unique in the solar system. The other planets appear to have little if any free oxygen in their atmospheres, and without atomic or diatomic oxygen there can be of course no triatomic ozone barrier. Mars, as noted, apparently has little natural protection from ultraviolet radiation; probably Venus also lacks an ozone barrier; and for one reason or another Mercury, the five outer planets, the many satellites, and the innumerable asteroids, comets, and meteors are all without gaseous oxygen. As a consequence they are all without life as we know it.

There is, however, the possibility of anaerobic (oxygen-free) life for which the energy associated with fermentation substitutes for oxygen combustion. Under the water and land surfaces, protected from ultraviolet radiation, there may be some biochemical evolution of living organisms that survive and multiply without oxygen. In the absence of light, ozone may be created by gamma radiation from the spontaneous decay of such elements as radium, uranium, and potassium. But this hypothecated anaerobic life does not seem very exciting or promising for a subtantial development of organismic biology.

If the Martian seasonal color changes are vegetal in origin, and are not caused by dust storms or by some sort of volcanic or geyser activity, we must contemplate a form of life on Mars that exists in a dominantly nitrogenous atmosphere, with very little oxygen and water vapor. Here is a problem for persistent laboratory investigation. In a nitrogen medium how little oxygen will suffice for seed germination and plant growth? This test should be made for various atmospheric pressures and temperatures. How effective an ultraviolet barrier would carbon monoxide and carbon dioxide provide? In Russia, America, and elsewhere investigations bearing on these problems are under way. I expect that photosynthesis will be found to work with much less oxygen than is now available on the earth—in fact, 1000 million years ago the then thriving vegetation (blue-green algae) had but little oxygen for photosynthesis; the earliest vegetation was protected from ultraviolet radiation not by an incipient ozone barrier but by the water shield, for until about 400 million years ago the earth's life apparently remained aquatic, safely submarine, getting its oxygen from the air with the help of splashing ripples and waves.

THE EARTH'S PRIMEVAL ATMOSPHERE

Assuming that the origin of the planetary system was along the lines of the modified Kant-Laplace hypotheses,* with a contracting central proto-sun condensing out of a gravitationally shrinking nebula with secondary eddies contracting into proto-planets, we accept

* The German philosopher Immanuel Kant in 1755 proposed an enduring theory of the origin of the solar system; 41 years later the French astronomer Pierre Simon de Laplace made a similar suggestion. The two theories, although not identical, are often referred to as "the Kant-Laplace theory." Both hypotheses have been modified subsequently, but their essential feature has been retained as the best available hypothesis.

the geological and geochemical evidence that the surface of the earth was hot a few thousand million years ago. That was before life appeared. We also accept, at least provisionally, the evidence that the gaseous envelopes of Venus, earth, and Mars rather promptly lost the bulk of their light gases.

We now know that the proto-sun was, and the present sun is, mostly composed of atoms of hydrogen and helium and that the sun has enough mass to retain those high-speed light atoms. (Massive Jupiter and Saturn can also hold them pretty well.) Since we reasonably believe that the smaller planets, certainly Mars, earth, Venus, and Mercury, were born of the same nebula as the dominantly hydrogen sun, we must conclude that our proto-earth, then chiefly composed of hydrogen, early lost most of its mass to space. The same would be true for the other inner planets. Our present earth is thus apparently but a small fraction of the original. We now inhabit a

✳ 93

planetary core, a remnant, with a mean composition approximately as follows:

	PERCENT
Iron	67
Oxygen	12
Silicon	7
Nickel	4
Others	10

For Venus the composition must be much the same, but Mars's lower mean density indicates a lesser iron-nickel core, and less gravitational compression. The density of the moon is much like that of the earth's crust, with a composition as shown in the following table.

	PERCENT
Oxygen	49.2
Silicon	25.7
Aluminum	7.5
Iron	4.7
Calcium	3.4
Sodium	2.6
Potassium	2.4
Magnesium	1.9
Hydrogen	0.9
All other	1.7

These figures refer to the outermost 25 miles of the earth, and the percentages naturally vary somewhat from place to place.

Hydrogen here makes a poor showing, and helium does not even place. Although in the ocean hydrogen amounts to more than 10 percent by weight, in and on the whole earth's crust it is only 0.9 percent, while hydrogen and helium, as we have seen, constitute more than 99 percent of the sun, the stars, and the matter in interstellar space.

LIFE COMES AS OXYGEN DOMINATES

Returning to the matter of life from these rather amazing facts of cosmochemistry, I again note that our present atmosphere is not the original version of the atmospheric blanket. A. I. Oparin of Russia, J. B. S. Haldane of England, and now many others have come to the conclusion that free oxygen was not present at the beginning. The primitive atmosphere, as the earth's surface cooled, was composed of ammonia, methane, water vapor, and such hydrogen gas as had not yet escaped. Also then present was probably some hydrogen sulfide, some nitrogen gas in addition to that locked up in ammonia, and the carbon dioxide and carbon monoxide produced by the prolific volcanism of early epochs. If at all present, free oxygen was not there in appreciable amounts. It had been combined with hydrogen in the production of water, and with silicon and other elements in the making of rocks. A "reducing atmosphere" prevailed in the early days. Slowly gaining free oxygen, some of which was dissociated from water vapor by the unblocked ultraviolet solar radiation, and some of which was produced by the incipient photosynthesis, our present atmosphere evolved.

It was in these early stages of atmospheric evolution, in the ploy from hydrogen dominance to oxygen abundance, that life got started. One step was the impact of lightning on the thin organic "soup" of the shallow rivers and seas, resulting in the natural production of nucleic acids and of many of the twenty amino acids, some of which in turn produce the molecular aggregates that constitute protoplasm.

This transition from the inanimate to the living was an almost incredible sequence of highly improbable events, but in a universe containing more than 10^{20} stars capable of building planetary systems, and over a period of at least 10^{10} earth-years, almost anything can happen repeatedly. And obviously this unlikely sequence did happen at least once in this solar system, for here we are, the timid descendants of some rather nauseating gases and sundry flashes of lightning!

✳   97

5 *

Life and Hope
in the
Psychozoic Era

You are of course familiar with the chemical element oxygen. Its atoms, like all atoms, are exceedingly minute: there are billions of them in every breath you take. They are the fuel of life. If you should cease inhaling them for a few minutes, you would cease to be a living organism. We human individuals are two-thirds oxygen. On the average, therefore, each of us embodies about a hundred pounds of that important constituent of oceans, rocks, and air. We eat oxygen, we drink it, we breathe it. There are also within us atoms of strontium, carbon, hydrogen, potassium, phosphorus, calcium, and many others —the same chemical elements that make up the mountains, the pine forests, the seashores. We are indeed of the earth— brothers of the boulders, cousins of the clouds, and distant kin, by way of the chemical tie-up, of the fossil plants and animals that in times past took a try, as

✳   101

we are now doing, at biological life and persistence.

It is in appreciation of our animate and inanimate brotherhood that I present this discussion of the greatest theme I know—cosmic evolution.

Honesty and rationality must prevail in religion, as well as in science, I believe, if religion is to survive among thinkers. Creeds that are based only on the knowledge of the world that was available centuries ago will no longer suffice. Should we not continuously modernize our religions and philosophies?

At this point I should like to put a simple but basic question—a rhetorical question. Continually our eyes are opened wider; the depth of our vision is increased. We see that stars evolve, that planetary surfaces like that of our earth change with the flowing of time. We learn that primitive plants and elementary animals develop through the ages into complicated organisms, including those with high sensitivity to their environment. Man, too, has evolved and so have his social organizations. Why, then (this is my question), should we not expect the penetrating urge toward change that permeates the universe to include the growth of man's groping philosophies? The answer is that we do expect it; to some extent we witness it. And we note that evolution itself evolves!

Some years ago the Pope, the spiritual leader of some hundreds of millions of Catholics, made an epochal address in opening a session of the Vatican Academy of Sciences. (The Vatican, by the way, operates one of the most effective observatories in Europe.) In that address, copies of which in five languages have been widely distributed, the Pope subscribed in detail to the findings of modern physics and astronomy. He made an excellent presentation of current atomic science. The age of the earth was noted as a few thousand *million* years. Atomic transmutations were described, scientific methodology was endorsed, and relativity theories accepted. That address seemed to me to make a very important adjustment of a great religion to our developing knowledge of the world and of man's place in it. Here was a most welcome indication that church teaching can also evolve.

A related practical question asks if the techniques of psychotherapy cannot be usefully applied in the study and interpretation of that sometimes dim and mysterious urge in man that we call religion.

In this essay cosmic evolution is our central theme; anthropocentrism is our trouble. If we could accept the former, and forever get away from the latter, our religions and philosophies would be richer and more honest. By anthropocentrism I mean the state of being blinded by our presumption of man's cosmic importance—our presumption that we are existing in a universe centered on the terrestrial genus *Homo.* Once we are free from the man-center illusion, our minds can roam over a universe that in size and power puts our inherited vanities to shame.

Let us review the situation of mankind in the presently recognized physical universe. When our killer-ape ancestor of a couple of million years ago battered in the skulls of the baboons in his search for brains and otherwise disported himself in the African caves and jungles, it is reasonable to surmise that his philosophical thoughts rarely rose above the primal ponderings about food, security, and procreation. Little need had he for ruminations concerning the meaning of life. His sense organs and interpretive brain were not attuned to ethical systems. He lived an ape life in an apocentric universe.

But the eventual emergence of societies among the primates made meditation advisable—made it necessary for long-term survival. Evolving man

began to think defensively and coopera-
tively. He began to observe phenomena
beyond the cave, the camp, the village;
and naturally, being nomadic in the era
before agriculture, he soon found that
much of the universe lies beyond the immediate horizons. His cosmos involved
at first a lococentric universe, with the
home camp at or near the center. As the
world's population grew and the early
philosophers resorted to thought and hypotheses that were based on many and
strange observations, doubts naturally
became widespread. There was doubt
that Athens, let us say, was really the
center of the universe. A geocentric hypothesis emerged—a theory, that is, that
the earth itself is central in the observa-
ble universe.

This geocentrism was a natural
enough deduction from current observations of the motions of the sun, stars,
and planets. They clearly appeared to
move from east to west around the
earth. The earth seemed to be fixed,

solid, and steady. But more and better observations gave trouble to the geocentric hypothesis; many adjustments of the theory had to be made. The idea of a rotating and revolving earth, with the sun at the orbital center, appealed to some of the more daring Greeks, although it was not until the middle of the sixteenth century A.D. that this theory, in Copernicus' version, gained ascendancy.

The stepping-down of the earth into second place in the astronomical hierarchy disturbed human vanity, but not too much so. Our sun-centered system of planets seemed to have a central position in the universe of thousands of stars, and to man that was important. The beneficent sun sends light and heat to the planet earth; that operation also seemed to give both earth and sun high significance in the universe.

During nearly four centuries the heliocentric hypothesis prevailed, in spite of the fact that the sun was soon found to be just one of the stars, and not impressively large in size or outsanding in its radiation power.

If human vanity had suffered somewhat when the center of things was moved from earth to sun, however, a bigger shock came from the discovery a few decades ago that heliocentrism also had to be abandoned as a cosmology. The center of the universe was no longer considered to be at or near the sun. The center of the wheel-shaped galaxy of stars was found to be some 200 million billion miles from the earth. The sun and its planets were thus found to be peripheral, far off center in a stellar organization—our galaxy—that contains more than a hundred thousand million stars. An equally amazing discovery revealed that there are billions of other galaxies, and that the sun is a typical star.

In view of these recent unquestioned discoveries about the universe, supplemented by the knowledge that the overall system of galaxies is expanding at a terrific rate, where now is man? What of his place in the material universe?

Since the new cosmic revelations have opened a physical universe that dwarfs what was believed a century ago, I propose that man now has something to make him proud and at the same time humble. His reach outward was multiplied a millionfold; and in the other direction, toward the amazingly minute, he has opened among the atoms a microcosmos of dazzling complexity.

Am I not right in suggesting a new orientation—in asking for a religious philosophy that encompasses the newly known, and which is not continuously in retreat? And am I not right in asking for the abandonment of a one-planet religion and a one-planet deity?

Because of its confused meaning, perhaps we should abandon the deity concept altogether. Should we not look deeply and sympathetically for religious beliefs that are founded on science, and that grow with science?

✳ 109

We should remember that the rule books (bibles) of most of the established major religions were compiled before much was known about the universe, or about the foibles and mental quirks of man. In early days men were uninformed in the fields of psychology, physics, chemistry, geology, and anthropology. We are still not overwise in these fields, but our present knowledge is far advanced compared with that of the ancient tellers of the "Holy Tales" and the ancient writers of the "Holy Writs." Are not many of our religious creeds becoming fossilized?

Today in a thousand churches—perhaps ten thousand—solemn men still arise and in public do what they would not permit of their children: they promote "false witnessing"—they violate the Ninth Commandment. Why do they do it? They make or read prayers of a vain character—not simple thanks for friends, health, and sunsets, but greedy supplications for special favors. Fancy asking, in the interest of one feeble primate on a small planet in a world of multillions of planets, that God give special services! It would seem utterly ridiculous but for the probability that much of the requesting of special services is not done seriously. It is a gambit, a venture. It often involves a quiet plan for cooperation with God. To many it is symbolic only; to many others, however, it is a desperate grasp at things eternal.

Although it may not seem to you to be a full definition of God, it is to many quite satisfying to equate nature and God. The phrase, now almost too well known, that "All Nature is God and all God is Nature" is a pantheistic statement that is quite operable. A shorter version is "Nature is God and God is Nature." Still shorter, and deeply meaningful, is "Nature is All!" That last is the essence of natural piety.

Let me speak more directly of cosmic evolution. The basic entities are commonly recognized to be space, time, matter, and energy; the first two can be linked together as space-time, and the last two as mass-energy. It is difficult to isolate any universal quality that is not a variation on these four. Speed, weight, light, distance, momentum, and the like are all derivatives of the four, or combinations, or are not universal. But would not some additional entity be necessary if you had the assignment of creating a universe? How about vague abstractions like drive, direction, consciousness, original breath of life (administered by God) , or cosmic evolution?

That last may be the fifth entity for which we seek, and which we need if a complete dynamic universe is to be established—if we are to produce a *going* universe.

The word evolution is commonly associated with evolving plants and animals, nothing else. It suggests changes in the biological world—for example, the wolf-to-dog ploy, the grass-to-grain development, the man-and-monkey business. Yet for a century scientists have been aware of evolution beyond the biological kingdom. We have seen that volcanic action and the oxidizing of lava rocks indicate that this planet's surface still changes with time; it evolves, and our atmosphere does also. The variety among stars suggests stellar evolution. For half a century we have realized that the fact that our sun is shining is evidence that it is steadily losing mass-energy (4 million tons a second) and therefore that it is evolving. Similarly, therefore, star shine must mean stellar evolution, a much mightier operation than we can muster among the animals and plants and noncellular organisms on the earth's surface. It is only a short step from stellar evolution to galaxy evolution. Going further, we see that the discovery of the expanding universe indicates that growth, change, evolution affect also the future of the galaxy of galaxies.

These observations and deductions

✳ 113

that a drive or major process touches both animate and inanimate nature lead directly to the concept of cosmic evolution as the fifth basic entity. But perhaps we should admit that this may be an entity that is not coordinated with the other four. Why not regard it as even more basic? Or as permeating all of them?

For the moment we shall accept cosmic evolution as a sort of fifth entity, but we shall not stop there. We shall lean toward metaphysics (that dangerous swamp) and reach for the most basic and permeating entity—the one without which all else is a vague nothing—existence. We could go deeper than existence and ask why existence exists, but the answer to that query lies in the realm of the unknowable and will probably remain there because of the relatively poor sensory equipment that we must use in our efforts to comprehend the universe.

To these vague thoughts I shall return later. Meanwhile I should report that the concept of cosmic evolution— the evolution of everything—has in recent years received strong support from new knowledge concerning the evolution of atoms.

We have long been familiar with the probable evolution of hydrogen into helium, and the accompanying release of the energy that operates most of solar and stellar radiation. (That simple atomic step in evolution provides for the release of benevolent atomic energy for the benefit of mankind and of malevolent atomic energy for hydrogen bombs.)

Is there, beyond the hydrogen-to-helium transformation, further evolution of the matter of the universe? The answer is affirmative. We now know how, with the help of the gravitational shrinkage of stars, which produces heat, and with the contribution of the violent energy released by exploding novae and supernovae, hydrogen and helium evolve into the heavier elements—oxygen, calcium, iron, silver, gold, and uranium. In fact, we now believe that *all* the chemical elements have evolved (and are currently evolving) from the simplest and lightest of atoms.

Thus we have evidence of a truly wide cosmic evolution from hydrogen atoms to *Homo,* and probably in some places to something beyond the *Homo* level of sentiency. We have in cosmic evolution a fundamental principle of growth that affects everything—atoms as well as biological species, stars, nebulae, space-time, and matter-energy—in brief, everything that we can name, everything material and nonmaterial. It is around this concept that we might be able to build revised philosophies and religions.

If, as we now firmly believe, terrestrial man evolved from the earliest primates, which evolved from lesser mammalian forms, which in turn developed, during the eons, from earlier vertebrates that had gradually mutated from simpler organisms, which two or three billion years ago emerged naturally from inorganic compounds like those that were built out of a variety of atomic species, all descended from the simplest of atomic structures, the hydrogen atom —if all that evolution occurred naturally, then a grand and basic question confronts us: Whence came the hydrogen atom?

There are many puzzles involved. Unsolved problems lie along the evolutionary way, but curious man may solve most of them. He may eventually learn or guess the parentage of that hydrogen which has as legitimate descendants atoms of all kinds, molecules of a myriad varieties, organisms unlimited, and man.

In our cosmographic survey we start with the mystical hydrogen in space-time and finish with the species of the hominid family that in our conceit we call *sapiens*. A deep puzzle at the beginning, and lesser ones on the way up; but

✳ 117

let us always remember that for the emergence of protoplasmic life supernatural forces are not required, nor divine miracles. Cosmic evolution naturally takes care of such matters as the origin of life. The progression is clear and rational through the whole course—atoms to stars to cells to man. But at the beginning and at the end there are still great unknowns; deep puzzles exist concerning the origin of hydrogen, the reason for existence, the destiny of the universe.

The destiny of man is not a lightsome topic. In the world of protoplasmic organisms he is an uncommon operator. The civilized variety of mankind is forever looking back over its shoulder (history), but sometimes looking timidly far forward (hope). Man seems to be unique in this respect. The trees and flowers do not bother about ethical principles of the kind that we fret about. The beast and the bug in this era appear to have no goals or morals that differ from those of their species in the Pliocene. They live according to a routine pattern; their programs are clear. Individual survival through self-defense, physical continuity and growth through the ingestion of familiar foods, and propagation of offspring in the interest of survival of family and species—these are the facts and acts in the life struggle of the bees and flowers.

But man, while sharing with other organisms some vital drives and immediate goals, has got himself into a transcendency where personal survival is not necessarily a major aspiration. He seeks distant goals that involve more than his own fate. The enlarged frontal lobes of his brain have brought the concepts and performances of charity, altruism, and mutual respect, and also greed, mendacity, distrust, and similar less happy qualities. These latter are human qualities, or at least they are more strongly manifested in man than in the less thoughtful and less scheming animals.

This mental complex, this forebrain of the most specialized primates, has so complicated man's life that precise programs for living now appear essential. And the program planning requires a philosophy of living and of life that we describe as an assembly of ideals. So defined, we can probably say with reason that ideals, programs for life, are indulged in deliberately by man and not often by plants or the other animals. Yet I do not feel too sure about this argument. Are we not rather hasty in asserting that the various artifacts and ceremonies of the animals, such as those of the social insects, are purely instinctive? And are we not equally hasty in saying that men are thought-guided animals in the face of good evidence that mostly we react rather than think?

The acceptance of the dogma that we, the higher Hominidae, are superior beings—an assumption based on our religious creeds and preliminary scientific analyses—strikes me as an indication of an incompetent cosmic outlook. Times change rapidly. Let us again look toward some of the horizons that have been altered by the explosive advances of science and see if our new cosmic orientation supports the superiority thesis.

The ants, bees, termites, and social wasps are highly civilized, practitioners of loyalty to the home, of altruism, and of brotherhood. But they are fixed in a sociological groove with little prospect of early escape from the rut of physical uniformity. Men also seem to think in grooves. Spiritually, however, we can individually be explorers, uncramped by grooves and barriers. Can be, but are we?

On this planet we are dominating among fellow creatures, but there is nothing to strut about in this situation. We are dominant only in the current "psychozoic era"; the giant lizards were dominant in the Mesozoic era a hundred million years ago, the cockroaches in the preceding Permian period.

These comparisons, moreover, orient mankind only with respect to the life forms on this one planet. We should broaden our views regarding life by forsaking for the time being this earth and its then superficial infection of protoplasm. We can then search for biological developments beyond our atmosphere.

Acting as your agent in computation and analysis, I find that the probabilities are extremely high that there is abundant life elsewhere. Perhaps I say that too dogmatically, but it is with the same assurance that I say, without visual checking, that iron is in the middle of the earth, that hydrogen atoms are wandering in intergalactic space, and that there is snow on the mountains of Tibet that I have never seen. Deduction is sometimes quite as convincing and reliable as ocular recording.

It is getting to be common belief that

in the known universe there are numberless planets suitable for the emergence of life. Our sampling indicates more than a hundred thousand million billion stars in the universe, and the number of planets may not be less. If only one star in a trillion has a planet that harbors life, there would be, nevertheless, a hundred million of them. Life is widespread. It evolves out of the lifeless as a natural product of cosmic evolution. Perhaps this natural evolution has produced elsewhere biological forms that excel in many respects anything that this planet can show.

It is not difficult to see how improvements could be made. For example, man has not enough well-developed sense organs to tell him what is going on. He has no good physiological register of long electric waves, and to study and use them he must resort to gadgetary feelers. He has no organs for sensing directly the ultraviolet or the infrared. Some stars have enormously

✳ 123

strong magnetic fields; our sun has a very weak one, and in consequence humans have no recognizable magnetic sense organ. It may be quite otherwise in other planetary systems.

As every anatomist knows, man is physically primitive in some respects, and in others dangerously specialized. His primitivism and his physiological oddities (brains, for instance) may eventually erase him from the earth. His clinging to the past keeps him most of the time at the wild-animal level—food, fight, shelter, procreation. His current reaching for heaven and the stars may disconnect him from his animal sources of physical and neurological strength.

We now recognize in the animate world only two kingdoms—animal and vegetable—preceded, some would say, by the noncellular Protista. Are these the only organic kingdoms that can be produced on this planet? On remote and happier planets there may be life forms other than plant and animal—other kingdoms of life. But have we not right here on earth the beginning of a third major category—the psychozoic kingdom? It is perhaps weak vanity on my part, almost anthropocentrism, to sort out *Homo sapiens* and say that he differs so much from oaks, oysters, spiders, and chimpanzees that he merits a kingdom of his own—so much that we can set up for him a separate set of natural laws, much as we can separate some of the rules for plants from those for animals. But vanity and hopeful wishing aside, the evidence is good that the forebrain —our large time-binding cortex—is of high consequence in the animate world and perhaps justifies the separate classification.

We cannot draw a sharp boundary to separate man from other animals. Certainly we humans developed from simpler, less thoughtful organic forms. The series is continuous from lowest algae to highest primates. But what may be beyond?

The future must be persistently exploited. We seem to be on the way to the establishment of a psychozoic kingdom, in which brain overshadows brawn, and rationality overshadows superstition.

I have almost brought myself to the point of believing that man is important in the universe. But we should keep in mind that this psychozoic development, this glorification of the human psyche, this rising dominance of mind has probably long ago been attained in other inhabited worlds.

Much as the free-moving animals outdo the anchored, sunshine-sucking plants, so we free-thinking humans outdo our ancestors, anchored as they are to their instincts. To advance further to hoped-for goals, it is clear that our emphasis in a program for life should turn away more and more from the animal—turn, shall I say, toward the angelic. If you are allergic to angels,

126 *

turn then toward the spiritual—spiritual in the broadest sense.

Where and why does religion come into the cosmic picture? Is it not one of the rewards and penalties of societal organization? Or is it merely one product of the restless human mind? Anthropologists report that all tribes, including our own, have religions of some sort, which are of varied intensity. Religion comes along with social habits and social requirements. It enhances the prestige of priests and chiefs and breeds a belief in miracles and the supernatural. We see and hear many things that we cannot explain logically; we make up answers to the sticky questions. If the answers are irrational, what of it? For such we can invoke magic. We can appeal to spirits. We can "get religion."

"Belief in spirits and things spiritual" is one definition of religion but not a comprehensive one. Another statement, from a famous philosopher, maintains

✻ 127

that "there is no such thing as religion—only religious attitudes." (That is not the first philosophical statement to make little sense to me.)

"Reverence for life"—the wide-ranging religion proclaimed by Albert Schweitzer. What a long way that attitude is from religious practices all over the world and throughout the millennia of human history!

To me it is a religious attitude to recognize the wonder of the whole natural world, not only of life. Is not the creed of Schweitzer too narrow, too selective? Why not revere also the amino acids and the simple proteins from which life emerged? Or why not go all the way and avow reverence for all things that exist, all that is touched by cosmic evolution, and reserve the greatest reverence of all for existence itself?

6 *

Thirty Deductions from a Glimmer of Star Light

IN these days when the high probability of much sentient life throughout the universe is widely accepted, it is natural to speculate about the possible kinds of living organisms and the intellectual heights to which some forms may have attained. Do some of the "beings" think more deeply and clearly than we can? Do the best have a better control of their material environment?

They must be good, we like to think, very good indeed, if they excel us in ingenuity, for we are masters in the handling of atoms, machines, biological cells, and the like; also in handling logic and mathematical analyses, and in promoting human conceit. Moreover, we are getting more ingenious all the time, and perhaps better explainers of the inexplicable.

What an enormous extent and variety of knowledge we can now extract from what appears to be so little data! Can the X-Statics on Planet X (which planet I assume to be associated with Star Y in Galaxy Z) do better than we can? That is something to ponder on. What do we mean by "better"? From the viewpoint of the corn borer or the pneumococcus or the dodo are we "better"?

In some small areas of knowledge we appear to have exhausted the supply of things to be known, and the X-Statics can go no further. For example, the structure of matter being what it is, and physics and chemistry the same throughout the universe, there are no chemical elements still unknown—we have identified them all, from hydrogen to uranium. We also know accurately many constants of physics and chemistry— boiling points, for instance, and specific heats. But there are still so many unknowns that surround us and permeate our knowledge that we could well be modest and admit that we may be mere minims in the over-all intellectual grasp of the universe.

Thirty Deductions from Star Light

Leaving modesty for another day, however, let us for the fun of it summarize the knowledge that is presently procurable from a pinpoint of light which we call a star. Which star? Any one will do: Sirius, the brightest, or a dim one flickering in the bowl of the Big Dipper. (The flickering is not a property of the dim star, of course; the turbulent earthly atmosphere causes the squirming.)

The Dipper's bowl looks very empty, but the large photographic telescopes reveal many millions of stars in the area which it bounds. More striking is the fact that through the bowl the Harvard telescopes have found more than 1500 distant galaxies.

Two additional amazing facts: the giant Hale 200-inch telescope on Mount Palomar could easily record the images of a million galaxies in the bowl of the Big Dipper; and since the average stellar population is something like 10 billion stars per galaxy, there are many more

✴ 133

than ten million billion stars in that small area of the sky.

Rather than explore further among these massive numbers, let us return to a consideration of what modern astronomers can find out about a single star. I shall list here thirty facts that we can now deduce from appropriate studies of a single star image. The first eighteen of these facts can be discovered about any star.

1. The position in the sky with reference to other stars.

2. The apparent magnitude (brightness) with reference to stellar or artificial standards.

3. The color index (found by comparing the brightness in various spectrum intervals—that is, measuring the color tint: reddish, yellowish, greenish, or bluish).

4. The variability in light; it may be zero.

5. The spectral class in two dimensions.

6. The variability, if any, in spectrum class.

7. The chemical composition of the stellar atmosphere and the consequent nature of the atomic transformations that maintain the radiation.

8. The approximate age.

9. Whether it is single or double (found in various ways) .

10. The existence and strength of its magnetic field.

11. The involvement with interstellar nebulosity.

12. The speed of rotation.

13. The tilt of the rotational axis.

14. The speed in the line of sight, and variations, regular or irregular, in that speed.

15. The cross motion—measurable only if the distance of the star is small or the speed is great.

16. The surface temperature.

✳ 135

17. The total luminosity (candle power).

18. The diameter.

The next eight facts can also be learned if the star is an eclipsing binary —a double star whose light varies because the two members of the system periodically eclipse each other.

19. The mean density of the two components.

20. The period of revolution.

21. The geometry of the eclipse—and whether it is total or partial.

22. The degree of darkening at the limb.

23. The ratio of the sizes of the two components.

24. The eccentricity of the relative orbit.

25. The inclination of the orbital plane.

26. The approximate distance.

And about a cepheid variable—a star which varies in light periodically because of pulsations—four additional facts can be found.

27. The shape of the light curve.
28. The period of pulsation.
29. The population membership.
30. The approximate diameter.

All these properties are obtained from the pinpoint of light. The mighty Greeks—intellectually mighty—could record only the relative positions and apparent brightness of naked-eye stars, plus the cross motion, color tint, and variability in very conspicuous cases.

Our great advantage in the analysis of a glimmer of star light lies in part in the enormous increase of our general knowledge in the past century, but in larger part in our development and use of technology. A partial list of our revolutionary tools, which are too complex for

✱ 137

description here, would include precision micrometers, photographic emulsions, electronic photometers, interferometers, spectroscopes, polarimeters, radio telescopes, lasers, glass technology, giant calculating machines, and numerous optical devices, among them Schmidt-type telescopes and giant reflectors.

Aristotle didn't know about such gadgets.

7 *

Out of
the Whirlwind

THOSE who are thoughtful about the history of science should read Job—I mean, of course, reread the biblical Book of Job. They would learn thereby how poetic the sciences can be, and how science-touched is some poetry.

I suppose that the greatest scientific poem ever composed is the *De Rerum Natura* of the Roman philosophical poet Titus Lucretius Carus, written about 2000 years ago. Some idle day I want to explore again his powerful and generally tuneful discussion *On the Nature of Things*. I first took a try at interpreting it when I was a college junior. It was my second piece of scientific writing of any kind, and I entitled the effort "Curious Lunar Theories of an Ancient Scientist." (By "curious" I meant "peculiar.") It was juvenile all right, adolescent in truth, but publishable.

In the poetry of science what rivals has Lucretius? Dante? No, for the *Di-*

vine Comedy is short on science and even on pseudo-science. Chaucer, Spenser, Milton, Tennyson? No, none of them; and Shakespeare was so indifferent to scientific matters that he does not even mention the Western Hemisphere (possibly he does vaguely in *The Tempest*), although America had been discovered—and exploited romantically —for more than a hundred years before Shakespeare stopped writing. Strange, it seems to me. I wonder what was the tavern small talk around the 1600s?

How about the Psalms as poetry and science? Not bad, but when we turn to the Book of Job, we are in big-time science, and literature as well.

As I read again some chapters of the Holy Writ, and what is written about the Writ, its origin and dating, I am reminded that there never was such a person as Job. He came from the land of Uz, the writer says, but there is no land of Uz—unless we settle for Uzbek in the

USSR, where today, at least, there is probably very little Bible reading. There are scattered mentions of Uz in the Bible, but where the writer of Job located his myth is not important. It is more to the point that this writing about the troubles of a fictional character in a probably nonexistent land is full of poetry and drama and imagination.

(I pause here to read the whole book again, and to check my persistent impression that it is a powerful drama with high flights of poesy and low sinks of misery.)

My favorite chapter is number 38. It contains, in the midst of fine imagery, a revealing survey of the knowledge and manners of Job by no less a surveyor than the Lord himself. This is no elementary quiz. I would call it a swift-moving doctoral oral.

Witness the grand opening of the examination:

Then the Lord answered Job out of

✳ 143

the whirlwind, and said, Who is this that darkeneth counsel by words without knowledge?

No answer. One is tempted to blame the darkness on the professors who have an abundance of wordage and only a preliminary knowledge.

We continue the questioning—that is, the Lord does, but with a warning to Job to hitch up his what-you-call-ums. (That is, by the way, the Shapley translation: the King James version employs unusual words like "gird" and "loins.")

And prepare yourself, for here comes the most profound question known to doctoral examination committees. The answer is really rather simple, but no one knows it fully—certainly not Job, confused by his boils. Here is the way the Lord put it:

Where wast thou when I laid the foundations of the earth? declare, if thou hast understanding.

Again no answer. When that question is put to our current graduate students, they, too, are silent. Silent at best; and on the average, dazed, for they cannot successfully reply, with or without a whirlwind. Some might venture: "I was not anywhere." But that is clearly wrong, for practically every atom of Job's body—mostly oxygen, carbon, hydrogen, and nitrogen—was in or on the surface of the earth when the foundations were laid. It is the same now. With the exception of some high-flying hydrogen and helium atoms, which have speeds fast enough to escape the earth's gravitational field, the atoms and molecules of the students' bodies were all here in Job's time, and also in the time when the foundations were laid, some five or six billion years ago.

. . . who laid the corner stone thereof; When the morning stars sang together, and all the sons of God shouted for joy?

What a lovely audition for the morning stars! Throughout this story of fortitude and suffering are many equally elegant phrases. But the most revealing phrasing, it seems to me, deals with the survey of the sciences as they were known at the time that the Job story was told.

When was the book written? I have consulted biblical experts; their answers range from 200 B.C. to 800 B.C. There is internal evidence that the fourth century B.C. is the most likely date. But whatever the date, we can fairly assume that the sciences of Job's time were well known to the author.

The questions cover many of the natural sciences, and the frequent invasion of dramatic poetry does not conceal the wide knowledge and deep curiosity of the writer. The examination was essentially a searching in the field of cosmography, supplemented by questions on piety and respect. The powerful cosmogonic question that begins Chapter 38 is followed by inquiries on geology, oceanography, and meterology. For example:

Hast thou entered into the treasures of the snow? or hast thou seen the treasures of the hail, Which I have reserved against the time of trouble, against the day of battle and war? . . . Hath the rain a father? or who hath begotten the drops of dew?

And then more about rains and droughts. And, of course the familiar astronomical reference:

Canst thou bind the sweet influences of Pleiades, or loose the bands of Orion?

There is great depth to the question:

Who hath put wisdom in the inward parts? or who hath given understanding to the heart?

Well, Dr. Walter Cannon of the Harvard Medical School wrote a classic volume entitled *The Wisdom of the Body,* in which he promoted the concepts of Serendipity and Homeostasis.

If we look over the dozens of direct questions we find that perhaps 30 percent are now more or less answerable— because there has been much progress in

✶ 147

the past 2000 years. The questions on animal husbandry, zoology, ornithology are now not too difficult, and concerning many of these matters the Book of Job contains succinct statements rather than questions put to the unresponsive examinee. The background is neatly laid. The Lord comments on the stupidity of the ostrich, and in the closing chapters of the book he remarks on hawks, goats, eagles, and especially on the war horse, which is so impressive that several fine verses are devoted to its eulogy:

Hast thou given the horse strength? hast thou clothed his neck with thunder? Canst thou make him afraid as a grasshopper? the glory of his nostrils is terrible [he snorteth]. *He paweth in the valley, and rejoiceth in his strength: he goeth on to meet the armed men. He mocketh at fear, and is not affrighted; neither turneth he back from the sword. The quiver rattleth against him, the glittering spear and the shield. He swalloweth the ground with fierceness and rage: neither believeth he tthat it is the sound of the trumpet. He saith among the trumpets, Ha, Ha; and he smelleth the battle afar off, the thunder of the captains, and the shouting.*

Beautiful, isn't it? Yes, that phrase "among the trumpets, Ha, Ha," is quoted correctly: verse 25 of Chapter 39.

Finally Job gets in his humble reply:

Behold, I am vile; what shall I answer thee? I will lay mine hand upon my mouth. Once have I spoken; but I will not answer: yea, twice; but I will proceed no further.

Had Job by his silence failed the examination? By no means. His humility and admission of ignorance was *the correct answer!* He passed with flying colors. For then answered the Lord:

Deck thyself now with majesty and excellency; and array thyself with glory and beauty. Cast abroad the rage of thy wrath: and behold every one that is proud, and abase him.

✳ 149

The pay-off was indeed most pleasant to that much-punished man, for:

. . . the Lord blessed the latter end of Job more than his beginning: for he had fourteen thousand sheep, and six thousand camels, and a thousand yoke of oxen, and a thousand she asses [that last item seems somewhat onesided].

And *He had also seven sons and three daughters . . . And in all the land were no women found so fair as the daughters of Job: and their father gave them inheritance among their brethren.*

What better could they expect?

8 *

Apologies to a Comet

written on the occasion of a celestial visitation

My salute to you, Great Comet of the 1960s. To you I shall direct some penitent remarks. If a few thousand persons should happen to overhear my attempt to explain a regrettable situation, it will do no harm. There is nothing confidential about the explanations which I feel I should make as temporary spokesman for the Hominidae on this planet.

As a comet you are one of the parcels of our common universe. You share the privileges of existence and of obedience to natural laws as do the stars, the planets, and the galaxies that populate space and time from here to infinity and eternity. We humans, collectively, are also a cosmic parcel. We have not had, of course, your grand experience with time and space, but we like to fancy that in some ways we are significant. At least we have a theory that because of "quality of spirit and quantity of intelligence" we are more than a biological flare-up on an isolated and insulated rocky crust. ✳ 153 biological flare-up on an isolated and insulated rocky crust.

We like the hypothesis of our importance—it is inspirational. But now at a very critical moment you disconcert us by coming by. If you were a short-period comet that came around regularly every few years, or a weary planet like Mars, you would probably know what to expect of us, and apologies would not be necessary. But in your unexpected call on this planet populated by boastful mankind, I fear that we may make a very bad impression.

When we found your image on our Harvard photographs, which are made with cameras that continually patrol the sky, and when, after some calculations, we found that you had come from the outer bounds of our solar system and would steadily draw nearer for the next several weeks, I was a bit ashamed and worried about the probable arching of your eyebrows.

To be sure, when first we looked at

you through our Oak Ridge reflecting telescope and saw merely a twelfth-magnitude blotch of nebulous light, we said, pompously "You don't look like much to us," implying, of course, that the observer looks pretty significant to himself. And why not? Has not the observer been able to build telescopes to watch you, and devise machinery for calculating your path and deducing, for instance, that at this moment, you are X miles away; that you move Y miles an hour; that you will be nearest the earth on March Z, and nearest the sun on April W; and that your tail is at least U miles long and contains the molecules of cyanogen and carbon monoxide? The observer does sound important and significant.

But then came the reaction. This observer recalls that the human race is not doing so well; that it is beset with madness, with absurdities that do no credit to a gifted animal that has had a million years of experience with nature, and with his own flesh and his own brain. I resolved to offer apologies, to offer explanations, and to make some promises on behalf of humanity.

It may be mysticism on my part, or just silly, but I should like to consider you, Mr. Comet, as a representative of Nature, or of the god of the universe, critically looking over the human experiment on the earth, on this No. 3 planet of this solar system. You are Nature's inspector, and I am accepting some responsibility for the report that may get into your cometary files.

When, some hundreds of thousands of years ago, you last came to this inner part of the solar system and looked us over in the yellowish light that our planet was then reflecting from our sun, we humans were not so dominant on the surface of the earth as we are now. The forests were more extensive, the lands and rivers less regimented, when you were last here.

I do not apologize for our defacement

of the lovely landscape because our earth is still less desolate than is Mars or the moon. Moreover, we have created beauty in a small way here and there.

I suspect that you found us happier in those long-ago days, at least in an animal sort of way. You found us, many of us, spiritually primitive, yet confident of the greatness of man.

The picture now is ghastly, and it is very hard to explain why, either in general or in detail. If you ask why men now have to strive bitterly for food when there is or could be plenty for all, or destroy each other and each other's homes, I might weakly reply that it is instinctive to fight, that we enjoy fighting and are willing to pay the prices. But if you ask me why we do not turn our instinctive combativeness to fighting against diseases, or warring with competing animals like mosquitoes, flies, and germs, or fighting ignorance or weak-mindedness, I cannot answer well.

If you ask why we spend more in material and labor on a missile of ephemeral nature, designed chiefly for murderous uses, than we would spend in founding a great university of an enduring nature, designed chiefly for cultural and spiritual uses, I can only admit confusion. Our minds and souls are somehow disjointed. We are too young to have cosmic balance or to have established objectivity with respect to mankind. We are still children in economics, and adolescents in common sense.

It must be difficult for a comet to appreciate hysteria. And still more difficult to understand why hysteria can be exceedingly profitable, financially and politically. (Hysteria is more profitable, of course, if it is steadily incited while its existence is as steadily denied.)

Perhaps the explanation is something like this: Our natures lack the dreamy calm of grass and trees.

Or is this it? Our books have told us that physical and social evolution comes

158 ✳

through strife, competition, conflict, and we are, at the moment of your call, striving to evolve!

Or how is this? There was some mismanagement in the past when our very remote ancestors ventured out of the shallow seas and drifted toward the plains and hills. On the way to the hinterland, property was acquired and so-called property *rights* were devised. Some of the acquisitive humans have systematically acquired more shiny pebbles than others have, and because of this have taken to vain and flattering reasonings about themselves.

Just now, Mr. Comet, we are awkwardly redistributing the shiny pebbles with the hope that we shall grow up, godward, with emphasis not so much on pebbles as on units of the non-material, such as units of pure knowledge, quanta of feeling, and measures of spirituality.

A comet has a simple life, its activities impelled by gravitation and radiation,

✳ 159

and perhaps by a little chemical reaction. But we primates are hopelessly complicated and messy, impelled by the same laws that a comet obeys but often rebelling against them.

And we have other half-known laws working on our bodies and minds, complicating our behavior, interrupting our progress. This half-knownness of our own natures may be our chief handicap.

You comets go smoothly, inevitably, toward ultimate dispersion and extinction, but we, babes that we are, aim toward integration and eternal life. We may be aiming badly at the present time, but the species is permeated with ideals. The human cortex may be top-heavy, and we do still reek of the jungle; we are perhaps rushing upward too rapidly. We forget sometimes that our fine brains and soaring spirits must ride in the same coarse body that our unskilled and uninformed ancestors used.

But isn't this rush starward a petty thing for you comets to watch, especially you who come here rarely and briefly in highly eccentric orbits? You can observe our struggles, our balancing of caution against progress; you can learn that some individuals on this earth say, "Let's make no change, please; let's preserve Our Way of Life," not remembering that the Great Apes said the same thing a million years ago, and great apes are they still!

Yes, it must be the half-knowledge we have concerning basic laws of Nature that confuses our cosmic program and threatens us with disaster. The human orbit does not yet yield to precise calculation. The available formulas lack essential terms, even for approximate solutions of the behaviors and emotions. These necessary additional laws of Nature are now faintly glimpsed, but not grasped.

Therefore I apologize for the suicidal man-eat-man operation that curses our species during your present inspection tour; but with some pride I point to our

✳ 161

current knowledge of galaxies, of stars, and comets. I am naturally ashamed of the temporary failure of our ethical systems, but I am not ashamed of our medical conquests and our understanding of the human body.

Our greed and frauds may disgust you, but look at our art and music and charity.

We could wish that, before you circle the sun this time and, outward bound, dim into nothingness in the star-rich sky, we might give evidence that the madness is passing, and that the millions of us struggling inhumans would show signs of rising from our deep disgraces. But there are twisted mentalities among us; whole nations are neurotic; we need a cosmic psychiatrist. Our own social doctors are helpless. They are merely medicine men. They go about the land chanting and dancing, hoping that the populace will accept and believe in the social brew that they have mixed for us but do not themselves comprehend.

Apologies to a Comet

I am appealing to you, Mr. Comet, as the agent of inexorable Nature, which has ruthlessly wiped out thousands of biological failures on this planet and relegated their annals to the fossiliferous rocks; which tolerates the continuity of a life stream only if it adjusts itself to progress and change—to change arising from the great rhythms of geology, to change arising from the growth and decay of fellow biological forms, to change in the physical and mental nature of the species itself.

Please mention in your report that if Nature will this time overlook our present relapse from the instinctive upwardness of our species and will administer the current heavy punishment only as a therapeutic measure, not as a preliminary to writing us off as another miserable misbegotten biological adventure; if Nature will have patience and give us the opportunity to square our spiritual shoulders and to sketch out more clearly a balanced design of living as individuals, as nations, and as a species—I promise that we shall do better!

We shall take better care of the mind of man, the subtle, half-baked, screwy mind of man; we shall try to bring biological evolution into better harmony with instinct, with metabolic process, and with the winds of the earth and the galaxies of the sky. I promise that if Nature will be generous and forgive a little the present miserable showing, we shall yet justify the large investment in mankind.

Yes, we may improve. If you return, Mr. Comet, and look in on us some hundreds of thousands of years from now, the scene may be more agreeable. That is our hope, and the basis of our request for time to get our affairs in better order.

When you look in again there will probably be some kind of world state here on Planet No. 3, hopefully with human personality preserved. National boundaries will then be gone, and our dialects amalgamated into a grand world language. Our dominance over this earthly fragment of the physical universe will then be based on a common recognition of our relatively high place in the world, and of our exceptional responsibilities.

We are well fitted for the assignment, we hope, by our distinguished inheritance. We have inherited much from physical, mental, and spiritual sources.

On the physical side we come from fairly vigorous mammalian stock—from an old family of vertebrates that has boasted throughout the past 100 million years many a strong back and crafty paw, as well as sensitive nose and ear.

On the mental side, we are really precocious—the prize exhibit in the Greatest Animal Show on Earth! There is nothing like us, except perhaps in the dazzling instincts of birds and bugs.

And finally in our spiritual inheritance—well, we act as though descended from angels *and* devils. This must be straightened out, Mr. Comet, but not before you pass near us late in the present winter. It will take time, and our apologies are now tendered along with the petition that the mortgage be not foreclosed on the human race.

9 *

The Five Beasts
of My Own
Apocalypse

a lay sermon to the young-minded

THIS is a call to war against the enemies of civilization. It is not concerned with dictators, or "containment," or bombs, whether A or H. It is rather a recording of militant thoughts, and a kind of double talk, for I shall speak as a schizo.

Part of the time I shall be a bold, cold cosmogonist—daring performer under the big cosmic tent. In my fancy I shall spin the planets, juggle with the galaxies, and ropewalk on the whiskers of the cosmos. The rest of the time I shall be a timid social scientist, searching for nostrums to appease the pains that afflict society, searching for survival therapies, and feeling sympathetically the faltering pulse of humanity.

I address myself to the young scientist, whatever his age; it is his spirit that must be freshened, not his calendar. Ours is an uneasy society. We ask what the role of the fresh-minded scientist is in this nervous world.

We should start with some definitions. Let us define science to include the social as well as the natural sciences. By "uneasy society" we simply mean the *status quo,* which is best defined as "the mess we are now in." In defining "world," the astronomer, who is sensitive to the humanity around him, goes somewhat schizophrenic. Professionally he would mean by "world" the whole material universe of which this planet is but a trivial speck; but unprofessionally he joins the non-astronomer in defining "world" as the human society on the surface of this one planet.

First I put on my skullcap, open the shutters of my dome, and sail my mind out into space so far that the taint of terrestrialism, the errors of egocentrism, the illusions of human grandeur, all fade away. From such a cosmic outpost I get the objectivity that is necessary if the world of men is to be located and properly oriented in the world of worlds.

In my mind's eyes and ears and reasoning lobes, I find that the cosmos is built on at least two pairs of fundamental entities—time and space, matter and energy—and perhaps bound together with the amalgam of natural logic. There may appear to be other fundamentals, but all of the many I know are but derivatives of these five: time, space, matter, energy, natural logic. They are basically and naturally non-human entities. There are other concepts that are widely discussed—such as life essence, consciousness, "the urge"—but these are merely combinations and complications of matter and energy in the space-time complex. Though earlier in this book I said that cosmic evolution was a possible fifth entity, I am now more convinced that natural logic might occupy that position.

From my cosmic outpost I see that matter is chiefly in large units—in galaxies. There are spiral galaxies, spheroidal galaxies, chaotic galaxies like the Magellanic Clouds in the south—thousands of billions of them. Refocusing my mind's eyes so that details emerge, I see that each galaxy is composed of many billions of stars.

For closer exploration let us choose one particular galaxy—call it galaxy 5,000,000,005. It is, we shall say, wheel-shaped; many of them are. It shows a spiral structure. Most of its billions of stars are in its hub, or in the spiral arms that extend out from the hub some 20,000 trillion miles.

Let us explore further, and search for "us"—for an animal that is currently in a struggle with his environment and himself. For success in hunting him down we must go still farther out from the hub, through rich star fields near the outer rim of this wheel-shaped spiral. At a distance of 180,000 trillion miles from the center of the galaxy we finally come upon an ordinary yellowish star that has, circling around it, a bevy of minute cosmic particles called planets and comets. On one of the planets—it is No. 3, counting them outward from the central star—green molds have formed; we call them plants. Associated with these photosynthetic molds are many detached forms that feed on the attached molds and on each other; they are called animals.

If I should make at this point an appropriate cold cosmic remark it could be to point out that if there had been different gases in the planet's atmosphere, these molds and the little peripatetics among them would not have formed. They got a break—these early plants and animals. The temperature provided by the radiant yellowish star and the chemistry of the available solvents were right for the necessary ferments and reactions. Photosynthesis and biochemistry managed it. Conditions might have been otherwise. The planet might have been as clean of such biochemical complications as are the boiling sun, and frigid Saturn, and barren Mercury. But the place and the reactions were right

✳ 173

for the experiment. Planet No. 3, near star, let us say, 4,000,000 or so, out on the periphery of one spiral galaxy among the billions of galaxies, is one place where this interesting experiment is going on—one place among probably millions.

A spokesman for the molds and mildews and ambulatory forms would call the phenomenon we have mentioned organic life, or just Life, with a capital L. He and other practitioners of Life take themselves seriously. Some are swimming, some crawling, some flopping among the vegetations on which they feed. Some are seen to exist as partially free individuals, and they seem to take that individual freedom with cosmic earnestness. They struggle to continue as individuals, apparently preferring that freedom to being a part and parcel of the much greater and more enduring inanimate world of atoms and stars. They boast of their individuality, but they are merely segments in a stream of life. The segments, or individuals, of a given kind, say, *Homo* (a kind that I pick not quite at random from the million types on the surface of this planet) , sometimes move and eat and fight and die in groups; they call thes groups society— human society. They have their own little rules, which are of course remote derivatives of the interactions of space-time and matter-energy. They are crazy, I suppose, or at least they appear absurd, with their illusions and delusions. They have a game called "For us the universe was made"; it is a song and dance with many variations. It is past belief how stuffy they are. For example, they get together and say, "Let's do something about the world, about the uneasy world." They say, "Let's put *Homo* in complete control of 'nature.' " They *are* funny!

Now I take off my skullcap and ignore the cold logic of a heartless universe. I put on my moral armor and become a

✳ 175

humanist, an uneasy social scientist in a troubled society. (I am of course symbolizing thousands.) Our god is humanity; our creed is effective participation in universal evolution. Our program is to do our bit to defeat decadence, to point out and assail the enemies that defeat humaneness and humanity, to incite wiser and stronger men and women to go clear-eyed into this struggle for the survival and progress of mankind. It is a really good species, this *Homo sapiens*.

From galaxies to human survival— certainly an ambitious program, you may think, and an inconsistent one. Is it not discouraging to contrast ephemeral and peripheral man with the apparently eternal and infinite world of the five entities?

No, on the contrary, it is part of our over-all philosophy of being. We must go along. Would we be true to the galaxies and stars, to the vegetation and animals, all of which also evolve, if we willfully refused to participate? Should we abandon the universal urge for growth and survival just because our knowledge challenges our wisdom?

It is a magnificent universe of incredibly glorious space, time, and energy. Let us go proudly along! Our social and spiritual evolution appears to be in our own hands; it does not await the slow flow of vast amounts of time, such as our bodies would require for a significant step in evolution.

The problem before us is emphatically practical. No hazy cosmogony and no fatalistic philosophy need deter us. There would be no sense in resignation. There are positive things to do. And nobody is as clear-eyed as the young terrestrial scientist and the young scholar and the young social worker. We now have or can find or invent the natural, artificial, and social tools for the human contests ahead. Also we have clear social responsibilities.

I wish we had as clear fundamental entities in the complex realm of human

✳ 177

behavior as we have in the natural world of natural science. Are there not societal fundamentals comparable to space, time, energy? Perhaps they exist and the more philosophical of us will some day reason them out of the complex motives of individual and group behaviors. Without them we must work and think in vague general terms when we confront human problems, or when we reason on the basis of uncontrolled experiments. Perhaps we can do a little better in constructing a working creed than to depend wholly on the ethics of the Christian and other great religions.

We could, for example:

Have some respect for property, but much respect for human life;

Have much humility, and much charity;

Have only a little self-esteem, but unbounded altruism;

Have reverence for the grand phenomena of existence and for the processes of growth in knowledge and in spirit.

The practical operations (ethics) for young scientists of good will could well be based on such a platform.

In America it seems clear that the international political situation and the mass psychology will make a term of national service an important part of young men's and women's lives from now on through many years.* Let us not regret too much the "loss" of those years at the beginning of adult life. Our fathers and grandfathers were indeed free of such interruptions, and these same ancestors (some of them) through research added much more than two years at the top end of all normal human lives.

We are now familiar with the volun-

* The Peace Corps was proposed and developed in the White House several years after the argument on the following pages was first advanced, and in part published in the *Yale Scientific Magazine*.

tary Peace Corps service. I am more concerned with a lifetime service, which would be in the interest of this nation and others. Nobody now believes that survival and peace, and international decency, can long be assured by a pile of American bombs, or by swarms of American superjet fighters, or by thousands upon thousands of encamped American boys. No, the long-range solution is not attained by those forced devices. They will perhaps check the sickness of world society for a short time. They will help very little, however, in bringing happiness and long-range security to the whole of humanity. They will not feed the billion and a half people who are chronically hungry, or shelter them, or bring the joy of existence to them and the rest of the world.

What should we do to discover and apply a lasting cure where now we use sedatives and astringents? One answer, which may be the true one, is now widely known. It lies in the establishment of a quiet and effective world citizenship—one that would carry with it a loyalty to humanity at large, supplementing our loyalty to home, to city, to state, and to the United States.

I am really saying (and here only in brief summary) that American participation and leadership in the international development of the world's human and material resources—development, not exploitation—is one of the great hopes of humankind. This program should be intensively studied by the uneasy young scientist. I am not thinking of those who prefer to turn their skills to profitable technology, making quick millions, and then cursing our country because of taxes. Nor do I mean the young scientists who want only to live a quiet and timid life—to settle down with a female of the species and bring forth young. No, I am speaking to the brave and inquiring who think beyond self. Such scientists could be members of a new kind of missionary band—fellow workers for humanity, servants to humanity at large.

It is hard and confusing, this program of world-mindedness, this devotion to world service. You may prefer to strive for that first million, or retreat with the wench to a timid routine, leaving the planet's society to chance, or to charlatans. But fortunately there are always some individuals endowed with conscience and with the spiritual yeast that leavens the whole society. Let us proceed with them as colleagues and workmen.

But before much can be done by the would-be doer, there is a vast amount of practical politics ahead of us, and the need of much American education in the art and practice of enriching the whole future by controlling the greeds of the present. There must be self-education also, and self-evaluation. Americans should be aware of their self-righteousness and deliberately curb it.

To Martians (I have put on the skullcap temporarily again in order to examine the situation objectively) the Americans must look fat and vain. They act as if they were internationally blind, for otherwise they would see that their best service to themselves, and their best assurance of nourishment and peace in the future, lies in present service to the depressed places of the planet. A Martian would be baffled by Americans killing Vietnamese, by Indians starving for food that others destroy, by such phrases as "Peace Congress," "fighting aggression," "containment." So let us leave the Martians to their puzzled objectivity and become subjectively interested in the five Beasts of my own Apocalypse and the methods of opposing them. We resume our moral armor.

The world-resources development program is devised chiefly to meet the world's need of calories. It is a part—an important part—of the fight against

Beast No. 1. Physical hunger is only one of the enemies which drive people into unsettling political programs. When we add to it the need for physical shelter (housing), we can name this first Beast Poverty and properly put it at the head of the list.

The second Beast is Ignorance, which begets superstition, which in turn leads to irrationality, and to the loss of the independent mind. Education is of course not always a step toward peace and progress. Some ignorant people are happy, and some educated people unhappy, but in the long run education pays, and we recognize that ignorance is a basic evil in a society that seeks to evolve.

The third Beast is Disease—an enemy alike of Russians and English, Argentinians and Alaskans. Here is an enemy that many can and must fight for the general good of all humanity.

The fourth Beast is Suspicion—baseless suspicion, the breeder of needless wars. It might be listed as a sort of disease; its cure lies not in antibiotics or surgery, but in the sciences of the psyche. For example, a psychoanalysis of Congress—what might it do for the world! And putting the Kremlin on the couch! We might save billions of dollars every year if we only could have modern diplomacy a-babbling on the couch!

My fifth Beast in this menagerie of the enemies of peace and humanity is Enslavement. Education, health, food do not make a man a man if he is enslaved by state, by creed, by economic system. The dignity of the individual requires personal freedom.

This point should be further developed. To the cosmogonist we may be nothing more than brief segments of a local life stream in the space-time complex, but to ourselves we are individuals, and beyond everything in the world we treasure our individualities. That is why we call enslavement one of mankind's greatest enemies. Some animal societies have evolved to a stage at

✳ 185

which individuality and personal independence are partially or wholly lost. The honey bee is an example. We have not gone that far—probably never will.

A principal cause of great wars, along with poverty, is our instinct to defend the rights of the individual. We fight against enslavement by political or religious creeds, and we are beginning to resist economic oppression. Without a code of human rights, or a good approach to a Bill of Human Rights, our spirits rebel, and eventually our minds and bodies join the rebellion. We would rather die on the feet than crawl on the belly.

The Martians, looking at our whole animate world, are no end puzzled! They mutter, "Those Terrestrials don't make sense!"

In concluding, I have an inquiring thought. Have we not uncovered here some social entities that are basic for progress, even though they are not

186 ✳

fundamental for life itself and for the continuation of society?

In the struggle for existence in this uneasy social world we have nothing that yields to mathematical treatment as do space, time, matter, and energy in the physical world. The human problems do, however, yield to spiritual and social analysis.

What might be proposed, we ask, as basic social entities? Are they not the antitheses, the opposites, of our five Beasts? Here are five social qualities that to me appear to be fundamental:

Material Welfare, to defeat Poverty;

Education in skills and arts, to conquer Ignorance;

Pandemic good Health, to defeat Disease;

Social Sanity and understanding, to withstand baseless Suspicion;

Freedom of mind and body, to counter Enslavement.

✳ 187

These are the five qualities, and young people of good will and good intent must employ these social therapies against the Beasts of my Apocalypse.

Again I name the Beasts: Poverty, Ignorance, Disease, Suspicion, and Enslavement. And the remedies: Material Welfare, Knowledge, Health, Sanity, and Freedom.

10 *

On the Prolonging of Civilization

CIVILIZATION seems to have few active friends. Who cares deeply about its continuation? Who feels for it sufficiently to be willing to work for its prolongation? We boast about national cultures, yes, and in an indolent, wistful, hopeful sort of way, these national cultures sometimes encourage thinking about the remote future of mankind. But nevertheless the world-wide set of interacting cultures which we like to call civilization seems to have a rather low standing in the thoughts and actions of those who think and act above the animal level.

A crisis has arisen in the career of *Homo sapiens,* which men themselves have created. Should they now attempt a rescue, or should they leave salvation, if any is possible, to those grand fates that also operate the billion-starred galaxies?

The survival of individual men is assisted by a deep biological instinct. We struggle naturally to live. And survival of the family is supported by a lesser but effective instinct. In protecting civilization, we go still further, for in law-dominated societies the worship of material goods is an acquired characteristic of some moment, now almost instinctive. But the long-term survival of states and national cultures is not instinctive. Only in a weak fashion is their continuation consciously pondered upon and planned for, and then chiefly as an extension of the survival programs of individuals and families.

We cannot now hide ourselves and tremulously trust to instinct and kind fate to save us. Togetherness now seems essential. This is not the time, and the earth's surface is not the place, for biological or societal isolation. The cave of the hermit lies on the road to extinction.

By what means could the indefinite prolongation of mankind be assured? Or put alternatively, how could man be completely eliminated? I believe the most potent of all the human genocides would be a combination of lunacy and war techniques. If one of our hypothetical supergeniuses of the future discovers a mankind-annihilating device, and this genius is insane, perhaps undetectably insane, he might willingly perish as he rubs out the rest of us. This is of course crassly speculative.

Noting an occasional overlap, I would list the instruments for human erasure as follows:

1. Pandemic superplague.
2. World warfare with supergas, disease, and atomic equipment.
3. Boredom, arising through complete standardization, or through the discovery, in a prolonged world culture, of the answers to all questions.
4. Drugs that kill the desire, or the ability, to reproduce.
5. And, perhaps most potent, the maniac genius.

What a battery of eliminators we have! Can we avoid all of them? There is a defense. To control the mad genius who might take the species to the grave with him might be simple: by educating *ethically,* while they are young, all primates that show evidence or promise of high talent. An expensive measure, to be sure, but because of the tricks stored in the human cortex, it may be the only way to save man from his follies for the next thousand years.

Although the survival of at least some specimens of the human species for the next few thousand years appears likely, the security does not extend to our present civilization, which is now endangered by strong physics and weak sociology. Scientists and converted diplomats have been hammering away on the immediate dangers. The frightful power of the atomic bomb suddenly awakened educated people all over the world to the necessity of heroic social action in order to prevent an unheroic physical disaster.

Although some of us have tried to point out that even without atomic war our urban civilization is in danger of destruction, the national worry has been centered around the possibilities of vaporization by atomic explosion and of burning and poisoning by the aftereffects of radiation. Many of us have been surprised that urban property values have not fallen drastically, and that the rustication of those who think of the safety of their own selves has not been more pronounced. Why haven't we moved out?

It must be, we say, because the average human being has an almost blind faith in the fundamental ethics of his fellow men, wherever located, and however conditioned by language and social heritage. Faith also man seems to have in the resourcefulness of his half-educated political leaders.

✳ 195

"Let us hope that the faiths are justified, but remind ourselves again and again that control of the atomic bomb is a futile gesture if the controllers do not recognize that many other things—such as guided missiles, mass TNT bombings, gas warfare, suprastratospheric rocketry, and similar engines of good and evil—must also be intelligently controlled if urban cultures are to continue. The hydrogen bomb is but one aspect of our painful future.

Since nobody plans to fight a future war with beanshooters or dueling pistols, it follows that human cultures can no longer be refreshed and inspired, as at times in the past, by the personal thrill of battle. The implements of mass destruction have altered that picture. We have the choice: war or civilization. We cannot have both. And it would take a long time for man to rise again out of primeval darkness.

To the explosive risks to which our civilization is now exposed we should of

course add those other mass extermina-
tors which ruin countryside as well as
city, farmer as well as factory worker.
They are the plant and animal destroyers that we group under the general
name of biological warfare. Their po-
tency, if used, and if quick defenses cannot be found, would be worse than that
of atomic warfare, for a surrender and a
peace pact would not halt their destruc-
tiveness. Their power and activity
would continue in defiance of political
"settlements."

These great dangers to mankind have
been so much emphasized in recent
years that I ask you to accept them as gen-
ocidal without further argument. We
are weary of contemplating the rubble
heaps that would represent our great cit-
ies; weary also of contemplating the
disrupted economy, the rise of mad
dictators, the ruin of the common life of
the common man.

The "scare" technique can sell tooth-
paste and soap, but can it sell righteous-

ness on an international scale? Perhaps
it can. But let us turn for a moment to
the constructive, the positive, the opti-
mistic. Some of the new atomic-age devices are as potent for the enrichment of
human life as for its termination.

Technology and pure science, if opportunity is open to them, can make
cultural survival irresistibly desirable.
They can tempt us to minimize, if need
be, the importance of our localized nations. They can inspire us to control our
national pride when it is obstructive to
the maintenance of a world civilization.
They can emphasize the new interde-
pendence of the nations, and reveal that,
in a new world, many of the so-called sov-
ereign "rights" are really wrongs. Science
has had experience in friendliness. It
could save us if we gave it full opportunity.

The social amalgam that is provided
by science and technology, by music and
art, is everywhere visible. Its cohesive
power in a peaceful world-society could

198 ✳

produce one of the finest constructs of modern man. How far we can go, in scientific fields, is hard to foretell, since prophecy in these days is myopic in the face of accomplishment. It would be good to have, a generation hence, a rich world that has not been decivilized by violence hatched from political pride.

Positive friendship for civilization, expeditiously organized and steadily maintained, would certainly not do harm, and it might eventually outweigh our dependence on traditional balance-of-power diplomacies. But the time is short. We must therefore steadily back up the best in present diplomatic compromise. Eventually nationalism may become less dangerous, because less discernible, and because less profitable to selfish leaders.

Given time enough, and good intentions, the psychologists, the psychiatrists, and the anthropologists should be able to explain our own social and mental quirks and teach us how to understand

and accept the social and mental traditions of others. Meanwhile we emphasize persisting friendships and tolerance —more correspondence across the borders, more collaboration across national political lines—until finally the boundaries are worn dim by so much international traffic.

The United Nations Educational, Scientific, and Cultural Organization (UNESCO) has high thoughts, great possibilities, and a fairly good program. Like the charter of the United Nations, this program can be improved and kept in step with the developing international problems and requirements. Can we not learn to rate vanity at its true worth and proceed to do on the international scale everything that cannot definitely be done much better on a regional basis? Can we not set up many organizations, institutions, programs, that are owned by the citizens of the whole world, supported by their good will and their tax money? Can we not tackle with worldwide methodology many of the worldwide questions, such as weather, health, food production, oceanography, radio communication, fundamental education? If UNESCO receives continuous and vigorous backing by the strongest nations and is kept truly international and as free as possible from bureaucratic manipulation, it can handle many of the future problems.

Next to the control of famine and disease, and the elimination of war desires, a planet-wide program for education at all levels seems to me to be the best way to prolonging a rising civilization. The Clark-Sohn program of World Peace through World Law may be an important beginning. This plan involves rewriting the United Nations Charter. It goes along with the general program of the World Federalists but emphasizes that World Law must be enforceable.

Even without the intermediation of the UN agencies, the scientists of America, in view of their highly favorable

*✳ 201

position in the world of learning, have a clear responsibility for leadership. They can set the pace, remembering that they are citizens of the world of all men. Perhaps they can soon cease to be dominated by a nationalism that can endanger civilization and discredit the technological world they have helped to create.

11 *

The Scientist
Outside the
Laboratory

THIS is a time of crisis. Most times are. But the present situation is not trivial. It is not merely a matter of crop failure and the foreclosure of a thousand mortgages, or a prolonged business depression; not simple as a political squabble between the "ins" and the "outs." Such human episodes leave the scientist quietly working in his laboratory. But this time the problem seems to be really serious. Wars are at large. Civil rights are in trouble. Should scientists do something about it?

Most scientists do not much like this out-of-the-laboratory life. But their knowledge and training should make them responsible to the public that supports their scientific labors. They must help to point out that the situation is not hopeless. They should insist that there is nothing incurably wrong with human nature. The chief difficulty just now seems to be deep in our methods of international conversation on the official political level. Diplomacy seems to connote disputation and contest. Diplomats thrive on failure to cooperate, but scientists cooperate automatically the world over.

There are more than five hundred international scientific and technical organizations. The members go about their businesses naturally on the one-world principle. They start no wars. They do not bluster, strut, lie, walk out of conferences, or rattle their big telescopes or their big cyclotrons and say, "Believe my cosmogonical hypothesis, accept my theory of neutrinos, or else!"

No, they invite others to join in the common use of their telescopes, to cooperate in cataloguing plants or fishes, or jointly to publish the constants of engineering and of planetary orbits. Science, like the arts, is not limited by geographical boundaries. Of course science is simple and straightforward compared with politics. The relativity theory, it is

✳

widely alleged, requires substantial intellectual effort for clear understanding, but its tenets are elementary compared with those of our multinational world society.

The scientist should remember, therefore, that outside the laboratory and machine shop cause and effect are not so clearly related as they are inside. In social problems approximate solutions must be accepted, with high probability of many mistakes. Geniuses among the world's administrators, and inspired social inventors, are much needed at this time of social crisis; and geniuses are in short supply. Before us, in a sense, lies a new world that we can accept or decline. Accepting responsibility may lead toward social triumph; declining will almost certainly lead toward disaster.

Do ingenious men of the sciences desire to devote the products of their ingenuity to human welfare? The answer is of course in the affirmative. But these inventive men of good intention must

✳ 207

overcome serious obstacles that are inherent in our social system. Otherwise their creations are futile.

In the capitalistic scheme, which we found very suitable for the development of our new country, we emphasize the merit of possessing dollars in large quantities. In consequence, the first obstacle to be overcome by the men who would work for the welfare of mankind is greed, their own personal greed. Too few of us recognize greed as an obstacle. In fact, the greed of individuals and corporations is regarded as a virtue. We do not like to call it by that name: we prefer words like thrift, wealth, success. And we are inclined to treat as un-American and subversive any talk about human rights transcending property rights.

But greed for property is not the only obstacle that today confronts the creator of intellectual assets for the welfare of mankind. He must also contend with the power and prestige of our military and bureaucratic personnel. This situation has arisen naturally as a result of the inflations and distortions caused by wars, hot and cold. Time may soften these power lusts. The progress which all creative men must encourage should not depend chiefly on the development of atomic power and atomic adaptability. Uranium, plutonium, and hydrogen have received an undue amount of publicity, glory—and calumny.

The atomic age was upon us, and our civilization was endangered by man's power of mass destruction, long before the first atomic bomb exploded. It was well upon us when electronics came of age, when the cyclotrons began to take the atoms to pieces, when the groundwork was laid for the rapid development of the sulfa drugs and the derivation of antibiotics from molds.

Even if the atomic bomb had not been constructed, our great urban cultures were in desperate danger from the development of guided missiles, jet

✳   209

propulsion, rocket planes, military satellites, proximity fuses, the devilish devices of biological warfare, and other developments now availabe for the technology of mass murder. The dangers of the age were upon us, and another war —the final curtain—had been forecast while the last one was still going on, and before the atomic bomb appeared.

But the developments of pre-bomb days carried with them the seeds of a new cultural revolution as well as the threat of destruction. The developments in electronics, fuels, aeronautics, and disease-eliminators had begun to make human living exceedingly attractive. The release of atomic energy has enhanced the potential for both good and evil. Its use has emphasized the dramatic situation as no other technical device could have done.

When the first A-bomb blew up, it took our complacency with it, and the bomb's flash illuminated an exciting social awareness in the ranks of scientists and scholars. The administrators and legislators in Washington took serious thought about the role of science in the national economy. "If science is what you claim it is, and I believe you are right," said a highly placed and powerful government official, "it should be central in our government's responsibility and not peripherally scattered in a group of miscellaneous bureaus." And many an American began to wonder if there were not a lesson, or perhaps a warning, in the systematic concentration of the Russian government on science and the scientists.

Outside his narrow and specialized laboratory the worker in science has both a new opportunity and a new responsibility. For example, here are some assignments to inventive men:

1. Devise psychological criteria by means of which the diplomats of one nation can understand the manners and methods of the diplomats of another.

✳ 211

We need an escape from the common assumption that because they do not do it in the American way, they are wrong. Such criteria will need frequent revision.

2. Devise an equable distribution system so that surpluses and deficits of food can be diminished the world over, and localized starvation eliminated.

3. Invent inexpensive methods for the transformation into effective fuels and palatable foods of the now worthless brush and scrub timber which covers much of New England and other wilderness regions. In other words, solve the major problems of botanical waste.

4. Plan political and social developments to employ the leisure time which technology can provide for all those now burdened with routine labor.

5. Create a widespread movement in crafts and arts, for home and community, that will elevate the artistic taste of the American people, and provide for

the discovery and development of the talented artists hidden among us.

These are serious and not easy assignments. Perhaps as a physical scientist I should be prophesying inventions in scientific equipment, not indulging in untutored dreaming, away from home in the fields of social and economic evolution. But why not dream and hope in all cultural areas?

We easily imagine sensational telescopes, lunar rockets, and space laboratories; also devices for boring toward the center of the earth in search of both knowledge and an eternal heat supply. We foresee new hybrid food plants, tornado destroyers, forestation of an iceless Greenland, and cows that produce calves in litters. Such mechanical and biological challenges are already widely discussed by science writers and idle dreamers. They are good, but not best—exciting, but not of top priority.

Man must act to control men. The greatest opportunity at the present time, the greatest need for creative skill, lies in the realm of worldwide social plans and devices that will make it possible for civilized man to continue to live and create on this confused planet, and make him want to do so to the full of his capacity.

The scientist has indeed a role to play outside the laboratory.

Selected Bibliography

The following are books by Harlow Shapley intended for the general reader.

Flights from Chaos. New York: Whittlesey House, McGraw-Hill Book Company, 1930.

Galaxies. Cambridge, Mass.: Harvard University Press, 1961, rev. ed.

The View from a Distant Star. New York: Basic Books, 1963. New York: Dell (a Delta book), 1964.

Of Stars and Men. Boston: Beacon Press, 1958; rev. ed., 1964.

New Treasury of Science. Harlow Shapley, Samuel Rapport, and Helen Wright, eds.

New York: Harper & Row, 1965, rev. ed. of *A Treasury of Science.*

Through Rugged Ways to the Stars. New York: Charles Scribner's Sons, 1969.

Index *

algae, *see* plant life
Algol, 54
amino acids, 19, 24, 97
ammonia, 24, 96
Andromeda Nebula, 55
animal life, 22, 24, 44–
   45, 83, 89, 101, 102,
   120–121, 124–125, 173
animals, prehistoric, 21–
   22, 26, 102, 121
Antares, 24
anthropocentrism, 104,
   125, 176
argon atoms, 37, 38, 44;
   breathing and, 43,
   44–45, 46–49; compo-
   sition, 39, 40; discovery, 41–42; in earth's
   atmosphere, 79–83
astronomy, tools of, 137,
   155
atmosphere (atmos-
   pheric blanket), 22–
   23, 41, 49–50, 66; ar-

gonic, 80–81; of earth,
composition of, 41–
44, 81–82, 86–87; of
Jupiter, 61–64; of
moon (lunar), 77, 78;
of Venus, 87; *see also*
argon atoms; breath-
ing
Atomic Age, 37–38,
   209–210
atomic bomb, 30, 38–
   39, 194–196, 209, 210
atoms, 35–38, 74, 81,
   101, 118, 209; classification and com-
   pounds of, 38–40;
   evolution, 16, 67–68,
   74, 115–116; man-
   made, 37–38, 49–50;
   weights, 28–29; *see
   also* names of indi-
   vidual atoms
automation, 14, 17

216 *

Index

Index

Index

ABOUT THE AUTHOR

Harlow Shapley, Director of the Harvard
College Observatory, Cambridge, Massa-
chusetts, for over three decades, is now
Emeritus Professor of Astronomy at
Harvard University. He has been the
president of eight national scientific
organizations, including the American
Academy of Arts and Sciences, and is
honorary foreign member of the national
academies of ten countries. The recipient
of honorary degrees from seventeen uni-
versities here and abroad, Dr. Shapley has
also been awarded numerous medals and
prizes, one of the most recent being the
Pope Pius XI Prize for science and humanity. He has made major contribu-
tions to astronomy in the course of his
long and active career, and his publica-
tions include half a dozen books and
nearly 500 scientific articles.